Informatik aktuell

Reihe Herausgegeben Von

Gesellschaft für Informatik e.V. (GI), *Bonn, Deutschland*

Ziel der Reihe ist die möglichst schnelle und weite Verbreitung neuer Forschungs- und Entwicklungsergebnisse, zusammenfassender Übersichtsberichte über den Stand eines Gebietes und von Materialien und Texten zur Weiterbildung. In erster Linie werden Tagungsberichte von Fachtagungen der Gesellschaft für Informatik veröffentlicht, die regelmäßig, oft in Zusammenarbeit mit anderen wissenschaftlichen Gesellschaften, von den Fachausschüssen der Gesellschaft für Informatik veranstaltet werden. Die Auswahl der Vorträge erfolgt im allgemeinen durch international zusammengesetzte Programmkomitees.

Michael Möhring · Uwe Breitenbücher ·
Alfred Zimmermann
(Hrsg.)

Herman Hollerith Conference 2024

Hrsg.
Michael Möhring
Herman Hollerith Zentrum, Faculty
of Computer Science
Hochschule Reutlingen
Reutlingen, Deutschland

Uwe Breitenbücher
Herman Hollerith Zentrum, Faculty
of Computer Science
Hochschule Reutlingen
Reutlingen, Deutschland

Alfred Zimmermann
Herman Hollerith Zentrum, Faculty
of Computer Science
Hochschule Reutlingen
Reutlingen, Deutschland

ISSN 1431-472X   ISSN 2628-8958 (electronic)
Informatik aktuell
ISBN 978-3-658-48214-5   ISBN 978-3-658-48215-2 (eBook)
https://doi.org/10.1007/978-3-658-48215-2

Die Deutsche Nationalbibliothek verzeichnet diese Publikation in der Deutschen Nationalbibliografie; detaillierte bibliografische Daten sind im Internet über https://portal.dnb.de abrufbar.

Planung/Lektorat: Petra Steinmueller
Springer Vieweg ist ein Imprint der eingetragenen Gesellschaft Springer Fachmedien Wiesbaden GmbH und ist ein Teil von Springer Nature.
Die Anschrift der Gesellschaft ist: Abraham-Lincoln-Str. 46, 65189 Wiesbaden, Germany

Wenn Sie dieses Produkt entsorgen, geben Sie das Papier bitte zum Recycling.

Preface

Dear conference participants,

thank you for your participation in the Herman Hollerith Conference 2024. This year's event covers numerous current topics relating to digital transformation with an academic track and an industry track.

The Herman Hollerith Centre has established itself as a teaching and research centre of the Faculty of Computer Science at the Reutlingen University in recent years. With around 350 students, multiple scholars and more than 20 doctoral students, the centre works on relevant issues at the interface between computer science and business. This includes topics relating to the Internet of Things, software engineering, business processes and service science, data and artificial intelligence as well as the development of sustainable business models.

The idea of founding the Herman Hollerith Centre (HHC) in the strong economic region of Stuttgart dates back to 2013. The centre began operations in the 2013/2014 winter semester with the establishment of the first Master's programme in Digital Business Engineering. Since then, the academic programme has been expanded to include a Bachelor's programme, two further Master's programmes and a doctoral programme.

The reasons for the success and strong growth of the HHC ecosystem can be attributed to various factors. Firstly, the HHC draws on the excellent brand of Reutlingen University with top ranking results in all relevant surveys. In addition, the teaching and research programmes at HHC address highly topical issues at the interface between business and IT. This focus is developed through particularly close cooperation with business practice and implemented in project-orientated research and teaching. Finally, the location attaches great importance to the intensive involvement of all researchers and teaching staff in the development of the strategy. Extensive third-party funded projects, first-class publications and scientific journals and conferences as well as a high degree of transfer orientation confirm this approach. Thanks to its first-class infrastructure and the strong support of municipal partners such as the district and the city of Böblingen, the HHC will continue to grow in the coming years - and this against the trend towards consolidation in the current German university landscape. With its attractive products and services, the HHC will continue to prove itself against the competition in the coming years. Innovative formats such as the Herman Hollerith Conference emphasise and support this strategy. Therefore, we are particularly pleased to welcome a number of researchers and industry partners to the HHC this year. These conference proceedings provide a very good insight into the conference. I hope all attendees enjoy the read. Hope to see you again soon at the Herman Hollerith Centre.

November 2024, Böblingen   Alexander Rossmann, Speaker of HHC

Organization

Organizing Committee

Uwe Breitenbücher	Reutlingen University
Michael Möhring	Reutlingen University
Alfred Zimmermann	Reutlingen University

Program Committee and Reviewers

Friedrich Augenstein	DHBW Stuttgart
Uwe Breitenbücher	Reutlingen University
Theresa Götz	OTH-Amberg Weiden
Christian Decker	Reutlingen University
Dieter Hertweck	Reutlingen University
Oliver Kopp	University of Stuttgart
Marco Kuhrmann	Reutlingen University
Christian Kücherer	Reutlingen University
Fritz Laux	Reutlingen University
Michael Möhring	Reutlingen University
Jürgen Münch	Reutlingen University
Peter Reimann	University of Stuttgart
Alexander Rossmann	Reutlingen University
Rainer Schmidt	Munich University of Applied Sciences
Katrin Schein	Reutlingen University
Sandro Speth	University of Stuttgart
Christian Schweda	Allianz Germany
Dennis Schlegel	Reutlingen University
Johannes Tenschert	Pertunity
Alfred Zimmermann	Reutlingen University

Contents

Introduction to the Herman Hollerith Conference 2024 (HHC24) 1
Michael Möhring, Uwe Breitenbücher, and Alfred Zimmermann

Academic Track Papers

Digital Platforms: Foundations and Future Directions 4
Rainer Schmidt

Towards actionable AI implementation capability
maturity assessment for SMEs 7
*Dmitry Kudryavtsev, Teemu Moilanen, Elisa Laatikainen,
and Umair Ali Khan*

Introducing AI to German SMEs – Practical Insights into Challenges
and Future Research Directions 18
Lukas Weiss, Michael Möhring, and Keshav Dahal

Realization of a Digital Product Passport for a Cross-Company 28
Carbon Accounting
Dimitri Petrik, Florian Härer, and Felix Schöllkopf

Generative Artificial Intelligence in Business Planning
and Financial Budgeting 42
Dennis Schlegel and Robin Fink

Exploring the Role of Techno-Overload, Techno-Complexity and
Involvement Facilitation on End-User Experience
in Utilizing Digital HR Tools 52
Soufinaz Baharestani and Hasan Koç

Potentials and Risks of the Low-Code Development:
A Systematic Literature Review 63
Stefan Trieflinger, Dimitri Petrik, Ebru Polat, and Bastian Roling

Developing a VR Solution to Enhance Physical Learning 74
Dominic Jungmann

The potential of generative AI in value-based selling 87
Victoria Sauter

Industry Track Papers

A Future Impetus for the Automotive Industry   102
Alexander Rossmann

Practical support for regional SMEs from the AI Lab Stuttgart   107
Lukas Weiss and Christine Schaller

Author Index   **110**

Introduction to the Herman Hollerith Conference 2024 (HHC2024)

Michael Möhring[1], Uwe Breitenbücher[1], Alfred Zimmermann[1]

[1] Reutlingen University, Herman Hollerith Zentrum, Reutlingen 72762, Germany
michael.moehring@reutlingen-university.de

Abstract. On 15 November, the Herman Hollerith Conference (HHC2024) took place for the first time at the Herman Hollerith Centre in Böblingen. The conference, organized by the Reutlingen University, consisted of an academic and an industry track, which provided exciting insights into current digitalization topics. The academic track of the conference included 8 peer-reviewed research papers on modern topics of different digitalization domains, while 7 keynotes about practical insights were presented in the industry track.

Zusammenfassung. Am 15. November fand die Herman Hollerith Konferenz (HHC2024) im Herman Hollerith Zentrum in Böblingen statt. Die von der Hochschule Reutlingen organisierte Konferenz bestand aus zwei Tracks - einem akademischen und einem Industrie-Track. Der akademische Track der Konferenz umfasste 8 begutachtete Forschungsarbeiten zu aktuellen Themen aus verschiedenen Bereichen der Digitalisierung, während im Industrie-Track 7 Keynotes mit praktischen Einblicken präsentiert wurden.

Keywords: HHC, Digital Business, Conference

1   Introduction

The *Herman Hollerith Conference* is the new conference for innovative research and current industry insights of the Faculty of Computer Science of the Reutlingen University. Together with partners from science and industry, relevant issues in the field of digital business are addressed. The conference took place on the 15th of November 2024 at the "Herman Hollerith Zentrum" in Böblingen, which is part of the Reutlingen University. The conference consisted of an *academic track* and an *industry track*, in which modern topics of AI, Cloud Computing, Digital Business, Car IT, BPM, Quantum Computing and Software Engineering were addressed.

© Der/die Autor(en), exklusiv lizenziert an
Springer Fachmedien Wiesbaden GmbH, ein Teil von Springer Nature 2025
M. Möhring et al. (Hrsg.), *Herman Hollerith Conference 2024*, Informatik aktuell,
https://doi.org/10.1007/978-3-658-48215-2_1

For the academic track, we received 22 submissions. To ensure a high quality of research, we selected 8 papers after peer-review for presentation at the conference and inclusion in these proceedings. The academic track consisted of two sessions. The first session was about the potential of artificial intelligence for companies including papers about challenges of AI for SMEs and the usage of generative AI in valued-based selling and business as well as financial planning. Session two was about digitalization, low-code, and user experience. Research about digital product passes, potentials and risks of low-code development, VR solutions for learning and techno-overload as well as techno complexity were presented. The research papers are included within the next chapters of the proceedings. For the peer-review process of the academic track, we thank all PC members and reviewers for their support of the HHC24.

The industry track consisted of 7 keynote speeches that presented the challenges, opportunities, and solutions of important current topics of digitalization in their respective industry domains. The first keynote about Autosar and GenAI was given by Steffen Krause from Capgemini. In the second keynote, Jan Wehinger from MHP presented insights about the transition from a Software-defined Vehicle to a Software-defined Company. Session two of the industry track started with Hardy Groeger from IBM about (generative) AI for the optimization and automation of business and IT processes. Guido Zockoll from iteratec discussed how generative AI will change software architecture. The final speech of session two by Clara Neumayer from AWS was about the *Amazon AWS Tech Alliance* and how to find IT talents in the future. Session 3 started with the hot topic Quantum Computing. Jan Trautmann and Michael Falkenthal from Kipu Quantum showed potentials of Quantum Computing and how it could boost industry faster than expected. Finally, Hischam Abul Ola from the Porsche AG presented insights about the important role of architects in cloud migration projects. Furthermore, in a separate session before the industry track, current insights into the usage of AI in SMEs and digitalization were presented by the regional AI lab by Christine Schaller and Lukas Weiss.

Academic Track

Digital Platforms: Foundations and Future Directions

Rainer Schmidt[1]

[1] Munich University of Applied Sciences, Germany
rainer.schmidt@hm.edu

Abstract. Digital platforms have evolved into sophisticated ecosystems that integrate innovation and transaction functionalities. Innovation platforms facilitate distributed development through modular approaches, while transaction platforms reduce costs for market participants. The evolution encompasses several phases: digitalization-enabled resource liquefaction and density, social interactions introduced user-generated content, AI-powered decision-making automated analysis, generative AI-enabled content creation, and AI-based assistant platforms. Each phase enhances platform capabilities and value creation potential. Contemporary platforms leverage network effects and artificial intelligence (AI), resulting in winner-take-all markets and transformed business operations.

Zusammenfassung. Anstatt Plattformen ständig neu zu definieren, um mit dem technologischen Fortschritt Schritt zu halten – wie etwa soziale Plattformen, KI-gesteuerte Plattformen und agentenbasierte KI-Plattformen –, ist es robuster und aufschlussreicher, sich auf zwei grundlegende Plattformkategorien zu stützen: Innovationsplattformen (die die Entwicklung ergänzender Lösungen durch Dritte ermöglichen) und Transaktionsplattformen (die marktbasierten Austausch erleichtern). Der technologische Fortschritt sollte nicht als Grund für neue Klassifizierungen verstanden werden, sondern als Treiber für die Bildung zunehmend vernetzter Plattformnetzwerke (Multi-Plattform-Netzwerke oder MPNs). In diesen Netzwerken kombinieren sich diese grundlegenden Plattformtypen dynamisch und erzeugen so höhere Externalitäten wie verbesserte Netzwerkeffekte und Komplementaritäten, verstärkt durch fortschrittliche KI-Funktionen. Diese netzwerkorientierte Perspektive bietet eine stabile theoretische Grundlage und praktische Anleitung für die Bewältigung der Komplexität und die Maximierung der Wertschöpfung in sich entwickelnden digitalen Ökosystemen.

Keywords: Platform, Ecosystem, Digital Platform, Assistant Platform.

M. Möhring et al. (Hrsg.), *Herman Hollerith Conference 2024*, Informatik aktuell,
https://doi.org/10.1007/978-3-658-48215-2_2

1 Keynote Abstract

Digital platforms can be categorized into innovation and transaction platforms, each with a distinct purpose. Innovation platforms enable distributed innovation by defining modular units for independent development, such as the PC/Windows ecosystem, where developers independently create software modules [2]. Historical examples include the printing press and the Jacquard loom, which use modular production approaches. Transaction platforms reduce transaction costs between multiple actor groups, as exemplified by Airbnb and Uber [6]. They digitize the functions of traditional marketplaces, such as Greek agoras and medieval markets, significantly reducing transaction costs and extending reach. Transaction platforms often exhibit strong network effects and " winner-take-all " dynamics, particularly in transaction markets.

Hybrid platforms, which are emerging in the context of digitalization, integrate innovation and transaction functionalities [3]. The App Store exemplifies this phenomenon, serving both developers and users who purchase applications, thereby generating substantial network effects and complementarities that are absent in pre-digital platforms.

The evolution of digital platforms exhibits distinct phases. The digitalization phase marked the transition from physical to digital resources, facilitating resource liquefaction (decoupling of information from physical forms) and increasing resource density (enhanced resource combination and mobilization) [5]. Subsequently, the social interaction phase incorporates user-generated content and leveraged network effects, as evidenced by platforms such as TripAdvisor and GitHub.

The decision-making AI phase introduces automated analysis and decision support, significantly reducing prediction costs and democratizing decision-making capabilities [1]. The generative AI phase further expands platforms by automating content creation, thereby generating novel forms of value and services.

Currently, the agentic AI/assistant phase is characterized by sophisticated AI assistants and complex workflows, exemplified by platforms such as ChatGPT [8], which create networked structures with diverse components, actors, and interdependencies. These platforms represent emergent systems of independently evolving platforms, as illustrated by ChatGPT's integration with KAYAK or Amazon Alexa's ecosystem.

Each phase enhances resource liquefaction and density, creating new value opportunities [9]. Future trends indicate increasingly integrated AI-driven systems. The distinction between platform types is becoming less pronounced as they incorporate multiple functionalities and advanced AI, leading to sophisticated digital ecosystems that merge innovation, transaction, and AI capabilities, thereby transforming business operations in the digital economy.

References

1. Agrawal, A. et al.: Prediction machines: the simple economics of artificial intelligence. Harvard Business Review Press, Boston, Massachusetts (2022).
2. Cusumano, M.A. et al.: The Business of Platforms: Strategy in the Age of Digital Competition, Innovation, and Power. Harper Business, New York (2019).
3. Cusumano, M.A. et al.: The Future of Platforms. MIT Sloan Management Review - Special Issue on Disruption. 61, 3, 46–54 (2020).
4. Gawer, A.: Digital Platforms and Ecosystems: Remarks on the Dominant Organizational Forms of the Digital Age. Innovation. 1–15 (2021). https://doi.org/10.1080/14479338.2021.1965888.
5. Lusch, R.F., Nambisan, S.: Service Innovation: A Service-Dominant Logic Perspective. MISQ. 39, 1, 155–175 (2015). https://doi.org/10.25300/MISQ/2015/39.1.07.
6. McAfee, A., Brynjolfsson, E.: Machine, Platform, Crowd: Harnessing Our Digital Future. W. W. Norton & Company, New York (2017).
7. Parker, G. et al.: Platform Revolution: How Networked Markets are Transforming the Economy--and How to Make Them Work for You. Norton & Company, New York (2016).
8. Schmidt, R. et al.: A Conceptual Model for Assistant Platforms. In: Proceedings 54th Hawaii International Conference on System Sciences (HICSS). pp. 4024–4033 , Wailea (2021). https://doi.org/10.24251/HICSS.2021.490.
9. Schmidt, R. et al.: Higher-Order Externalities in Multi-Platform Ecosystems. In: Proceedings 57th Hawaii International Conference on System Sciences (HICSS). pp. 3990–3999, Honolulu, Hawaii (2024).

Towards actionable AI implementation capability maturity assessment for SMEs

Dmitry Kudryavtsev[1][0000-0002-1798-5809], Teemu Moilanen[1][0000-0002-5784-2829], Elisa Laatikainen[1][TBD] and Umair Ali Khan[1][0000-0002-8560-764X]

[1] Haaga-Helia University of Applied Sciences, Ratapihantie 13, 00520 Helsinki, Finland
{Dmitry.Kudryavtsev, Teemu.Moilanen, Elisa.Laatikainen, UmairAli.Khan}@haaga-helia.fi

Abstract. AI implementation is a critical survival factor for all the companies. SMEs lag in the AI adoption and need a tool support for assessing and developing AI implementation capabilities. The analysis of industry needs provided the following key requirements for this tool: 1. Ability to suggest and select improvement actions (prescriptive functionality) in addition to the assessment of current state (descriptive functionality); 2. SMEs-focused, which is mostly reflected in the selection of maturity assessment indicators and emphasis on low maturity levels; 3. Completeness justification of AI implementation capability maturity dimensions. Additionally, the tool must be well-documented and available for use. The existing AI maturity models do not satisfy these requirements, so there is a need to develop a new tool. The paper presents an ongoing research project aiming to create an AI implementation capability development planning tool for SMEs (AICapDev), which includes a capability assessment part (the primary focus of the current text) and a roadmap creation part. The current paper presents the preliminary research results, more specifically for: (1) Problem Definition, (2) Comparison of existing Models, (3) Determination of development strategy, (4) Model development steps. Future research directions are also highlighted in the conclusion.

Zusammenfassung. Die Implementierung von KI ist für alle Unternehmen ein kritischer Überlebensfaktor. KMUs hinken bei der Einführung von KI hinterher und benötigen ein Tool zur Bewertung und Entwicklung von KI-Capabilities. Es wird ein Capability Model für KI Implementierung für SMEs im Aufsatz entwickelt. Neben der Entwicklung und Vorstellung des Modells werden in der Schlussfolgerung auch künftige Forschungsrichtungen aufgezeigt.

Keywords: AI, maturity model, AI implementation capability, SMEs, Design science research.

1   Introduction

Artificial intelligence (AI) is potentially one of the most important, if not the most important, technologies of the future [1],[2]. AI is expected to disrupt business models, create new ways of working and learning, and facilitate the digital transformation of societies. Companies are trying to implement AI into their processes, products, services and business models. However, the speed of AI implementation correlates heavily with company size. Similarly to digitalization, while large corporations are in the vanguard, small and medium-sized enterprises (SMEs) are largely just starting the journey [3]. Small and medium-sized enterprises (SMEs) represent 99% of all businesses in the EU. The category of SMEs comprises enterprises that employ fewer than 250 persons and have an annual turnover not exceeding EUR 50 million, and/or an annual balance sheet total not exceeding EUR 43 million [4].

SMEs face challenges integrating AI into organisational processes and products/services [5], [6]. The AI implementation capabilities of SMEs are often insufficient for defining beneficial AI use cases, designing needed AI solutions, creating corresponding action plans and implementing them with acceptable time, money and risk amounts. The assistance for SMEs in assessing and developing AI implementation capabilities would be helpful.

This understanding of SMEs' challenges and needs is driven by our participation in the Finnish AI Region (FAIR) European Digital Innovation Hub (EDIHs) (https://www.fairedih.fi/en/). FAIR EDIH focuses on speeding up and enlarging the use of AI by SMEs primarily in Finland. European Digital Innovation Hubs, EDIHs (https://digital-strategy.ec.europa.eu/en/activities/edihs) are key entities established by the European Union to support businesses, public sector organizations, and industries in their digital transformation efforts. They provide access to technological expertise, infrastructure, and services that can help accelerate the adoption of advanced digital technologies including artificial intelligence (AI) [7]. At present, FAIR EDIH provides services to approximately 130 companies, while our team provided needs analysis and advisory to 60+ SMEs.

The advisory experience helped us see the urgent need to navigate companies during their AI adoption journey by diagnosing their initial situation and needs and helping them craft an action plan for creating and implementing AI solutions. AI readiness enhancement is often a part of such plan (roadmap). Until now, we have combined survey-like AI maturity assessments using VTT's AI maturity model [8] with one-hour needs analysis sessions led by AI experts, where in-depth diagnostic and maturity assessments took place. The feedback from the FAIR EDIH customers and customer managers for the existing maturity model (the questionnaire is filled in by SMEs with the customer managers' support) highlighted the next following limitations:

1. AI maturity assessment using the existing AI maturity model raises the "then what?" question, meaning that the company knows its maturity profile but is unclear about what to do next.

2.   Some questions of the existing AI maturity model are primarily suitable for big and relatively mature companies; it is hard for SMEs to answer such questions, for example, about the AI strategy or AI impact measurement.

This feedback led to the following business-driven requirements for the AI implementation capability maturity assessment tool:

R1. Ability to suggest and select improvement actions (prescriptive functionality) in addition to assessment of current state (descriptive functionality) including: a) Generic improvement actions, b) FAIR EDIH services (specific for FAIR EDIH needs).

R2. SMEs-focused, which is mostly reflected in the selection of maturity assessment indicators and emphasis on low maturity levels.

Reviewing the existing AI maturity models and assessment tools raised another concern – some assessment models look fragmented and incomplete, e.g. addressing only one aspect of data for AI. This concern led to one more requirement driven mainly by scientific rigour:

R3. Completeness justification of AI implementation capability maturity dimensions (ability to justify the completeness or sufficiency of the model in terms of the number of dimensions, assessment questions, etc.).

The need for practical utilization of the toolset raised the final requirement:

R4. The model/tool must be well-documented and available for use.

The review of existing AI maturity models (MM) [9], [10], [11] revealed that no one satisfies the suggested requirements. So, there is a need to develop a new tool.

The paper presents an ongoing research project aiming to create an AI implementation capability development planning tool for SMEs (AICapDev), which includes a capability assessment part (the primary focus of the current text) and a roadmap creation part.

2   Analysis of existing maturity models and related work

2.1   Existing AI maturity models

Good systemic reviews of AI MMs are provided in [9], [10], [11]. These reviews provided the foundation for our work.

The requirements for the AICapDev tool were used as a filter for selecting and analysing existing AI MMs. Our analysis of existing AI maturity models revealed that no one satisfies the suggested requirements. So, there is a need to develop a new tool.

A fragment of existing AI MMs assessment with respect to the requirements is provided in Table 1. These models also provided insights for developing AICapDev tool.

Table 1. Comparison of AI Maturity models (with a special focus on the AIMM for SMEs)

AI maturity model	Strong points	Limitations concerning the requirements
VTT's AIMM [8]	Validated and implemented into open online tool Concise and easy to use Well documented	1) Improvement measures are not suggested 2) Questions are more suitable for large and relatively mature companies 3) The selection of questions for maturity assessment looks fragmented and incomplete
AIMM [10], [12]	Focus on SMEs, privacy, and ethics. Well documented	1) Improvement actions are not suggested 2) Lack of real-life validation (use cases with fictional companies)
AI adoption model for SMEs [13]	Focus on SMEs Improvement actions are suggested	Improvement actions are provided for each dimension [14], but not associated with maturity levels Focus on manufacturing companies
Maturity Model for AI Deployment Capability of Manufacturing Companies [11]	Well documented Dimensions are decomposed into attributes	1) Too many questions for SMEs 2) Improvement actions are not suggested

2.2   AI implementation/management capabilities

To have theoretical foundations for assessing existing AI MM and developing own tool, we reviewed the current work devoted to conceptualizing and measuring such capabilities.

Weber et al [15] suggested four organizational capabilities for AI implementation: 1) AI Project Planning: The ability to identify, evaluate and prioritize suitable AI use cases; 2) Co-Development of AI Systems: The ability to communicate with and integrate stakeholders into AI implementation; 3) Data Management: The ability to collect, curate, and provide data for AI implementation; 4) AI Model Lifecycle Management: The ability to orchestrate the evolution of AI models, including development, deployment, and maintenance.

Mikalef, P., & Gupta [16] suggested the conceptualization of AI capability, which has the following components: A. Tangible Resources (Data, Technology, Basic Resources), B. Human Resources (Technical Skills, Business skills), C. Intangible Resources (Inter-departmental Coordination, Organizational Change Capacity, Risk Proclivity)

Sjödin et al [17] defined the following AI capabilities: A. Data Pipeline capabilities, B. Algorithm development capabilities, C. AI democratization capabilities.

Fukas and Thomas [18] suggested AI management reference model: 1. Core activities: Technology and Infrastructure, Data, People & Competencies and Organization & Processes; 2. Value activities: Products and services, 3. Governance activities: Strategy & Management, Ethics & Regulations, 4. Enabling activities: Budget & Investment.

3   Research and development methodology

Since the desired AICapDev tool is close to a prescriptive maturity model (MM), we used MM development methods to guide our process.

Becker et al [19] suggested the process model for developing MM, which is used in our research. It includes the following steps:

1) Problem Definition, including domain and target group specification,

2) Comparison of existing Models to identify their limitations and reuse opportunities,

3) Determination of development strategy (e.g. new model design or enhancement of the existing one, transfer of structures or contents),

4) Iterative maturity model development, which includes selection of the design level and approach, creation of the model sections, and testing,

5) Conception of transfer and evaluation (defining the way of MM representation and use for various target groups, including the mechanisms for the feedback collection for the MM evaluation and improvement),

6) Implementation (e.g. in the form of self-assessment questionnaires, assessment guides, or online services)

7) Evaluation of whether the MM provides the projected benefits and an improved solution for the problem.

The current paper presents the ongoing research and addresses four of the seven steps of the MM development process [19]: from (1) Problem Definition to 4) Iterative maturity model development. The other steps (5) Conception of transfer and evaluation, (6) Implementation (7) Evaluation are currently in progress and will be presented in the future publications. The aforementioned steps were done iteratively, starting at the conceptual high level and then increasing the analysis and design details.

In addition to the process model, we will use the design principles for MM suggested in [20].

We used the following data collection methods and sources:

(1) Problem Definition was driven by industry needs and used: Interviews with AI customer managers, who do AI maturity assessment, plan and coordinate the AI journeys of SMEs; Documented feedback from SMEs that used another AI MM for self-assessment and diagnostics; Interviews with AI expert, who provides needs analysis and technical AI advisory to SMEs; Own reflections of the AI advisory manager;

(2) Comparison of existing AI MMs and related work – literature review;

(3) Determination of development strategy and (4) Iterative maturity model development: co-creation sessions, which included AI customer managers, AI experts and the AI advisory manager, and feedback sessions with AI experts.

4   Problem definition and requirements specification

The general problem relevance and the need to assess and develop AI implementation capabilities of SMEs were described in the introduction.

In line with the design principles for MM [20], we defined basic information about the AICapDev tool below.

Application area: Organizational capabilities for AI implementation

Target group (potential users):

1. Managers within AI advisory agencies/organizations, who can apply the tool to understand the AI implementation capability of SMEs and plan/coordinate the AI journeys of SMEs (for FAIR EDIH: customer/account managers);

2. Founders/CEOs/CXOs/leaders of SMEs, who can either use the tool themselves or together with group 1;

3. Training providers (including universities) to plan AI training portfolios.

Class of entities under investigation: SMEs from various industries that either develop (or plan to do it) products/services with AI elements or have knowledge-intensive activities with high AI utilization potential (e.g. consulting or law advisory).

We also formulated the requirements for the AICapDev tool at the problem definition step – they were presented in the Introduction.

5   Development strategy and design decisions

We used the following design principles:

1. Creation of prescriptive model, which can suggest and help to select improvement actions to increase the AI implementation capability, including generic and specific to FAIR EDIH ones (see R1);

2. The key concepts and development principles should be based on topic areas maturity models approach [21], [22]. This approach is effective for creating flexible prescriptive MM. So, the following process and key concepts were used for creating AICapDev model – see Fig. 1. Some modifications were done in comparison with the original method of van Steenbergen et al [21]:

   a. We use the term dimension in parallel with the topic area, as synonyms. Dimensions are suggested in many existing MMs, and they were reused for creating our model;

   b. Categories were added for structuring and completeness check of dimensions (topics areas);

   c. The concept of dimension attributes was introduced to formulate decomposition principles for each dimension – how to determine capability levels; Dimension attributes worked as a bridge for knowledge reuse from other AI MMs,

d. The term "capability level" was suggested instead of the "capability", since we decided to keep the meaning of "capability" closer to TOGAF business capability planning [23];

e. FAIR EDIH services were added as a part of recommendations for achieving each capability level.

3. Since we want to assess and develop AI implementation capability and the concept of capability usually defines what a system can do, we decided to select an established conceptual model for describing activities as a template for completeness check. It was done in line with an idea of using templates as a way of providing completeness for knowledge diagrams [24]. Structured analysis and design technique (SADT) [25] will be used to check the completeness (see R3) and organize AI implementation capability dimensions.

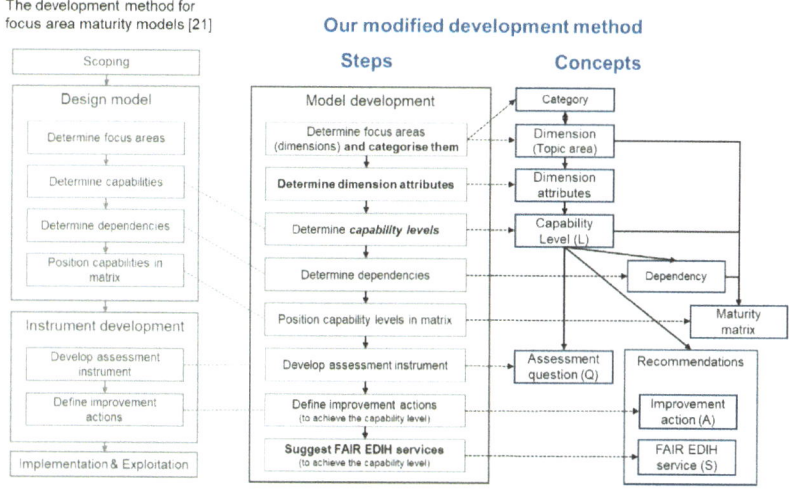

Fig. 1. Process and key concepts for creating AICapDev model

6   The core elements of AI implementation capability assessment

AI implementation capability dimensions were created based on the analysis of existing AI MMs and approaches for defining AI implementation capabilities (see Table 2).

Table 2. Dimensions of the AI implementation capability, their justification and grouping

Categories	Dimensions (Focus areas)	Sources
Activities (What do you do to implement AI?)	AI models development, deployment and maintenance	[15], [17]
	Data management processes	[15], [17]
	Co-creation of AI system	[15], [17]
Outputs (What you already achieved?)	AI integration into existing products and processes	[26], [27]
Control (How is AI implementation steered?)	AI use cases	[15], [18]
	AI Strategy	[8]
	Regulatory and ethical risks	[18]
Input (What data will be used for AI?)	Data	Many AI MMs
Resources (What resources do you have to implement AI)	People and Skills	Many AI MMs
	Technology	Many AI MMs

SADT methodology [25] helped to group the dimensions and provided a theoretical foundation for their completeness. According to SADT, the systemic description of work includes activities, their inputs, outputs, controls and resources/mechanism.

The description of one of the AICapDev-SME tool's dimensions is presented in Table 3, including dimension attributes (decomposition approach), capability levels, assessment questions, as well as prescriptive elements – improvement actions and recommended FAIR EDIH services.

The model/tool will work in the following way:

1. A SME representative/-s answers the Assessment questions (A),
2. The Capability level (L) of the SME for each dimension is defined based on the answers and table 3 (all positive answers to the assessment questions associate to a certain capability level = this level is achieved by the SME),
3. The most needed *next* capability levels are defined based on the dependencies between capability levels reflected in the maturity matrix and strategic priorities of SME,
4. Improvement actions (A) and FAIR EDIH Services (S) predefined by Table 3 are recommended to achieve the most needed *next* capability levels.

Table 3. Example description of one AI implementation capability dimension

Dimension: AI integration into products and processes of the company			
Dimension attributes (Decomposition approach): A. AI implementation level: preliminary ideas, POC, prototype/system with real-life validation, system in use B. Coverage – number of processes and products			
Capability levels	**Assessment questions**	**Actions to achieve the capability level**	**FAIR EDIH services to achieve the capability level**
L0. Only preliminary ideas for using AI in the company without actual usage of AI in business operations	Q1: The company has only preliminary ideas for utilising AI, but hasn't yet tried AI		
L1. Adhoc use of AI tools/services in support of AI usage ideas	Q2: The company has an ad-hoc experience of using AI tools/services	A1. Get hands-on experience with AI by utilising AI tools/services for business tasks (e.g. ChatGPT) associated with AI utilization ideas	S1. AI advisory service – To recommend AI tools and technologies relevant to the company's ideas
L2. AI-based POCs in one or more areas	Q3: The company created a POC for the promising AI idea/-s Q4: The company tested POC in the lab	A2. Create POC(-s) for the most promising AI idea(-s) A3. Test your POC/solution in the lab	S2. POC to test AI-based business idea S3. Advisory service – Requirements specification for the POC
L3. AI-based prototypes/systems are created and validated in one or more processes/products of the company	Q5: The company created prototype/system based on POC Q6: The company validated the prototype/system with users	A4. Create an AI-based prototype/system based on the POC results and feedback A5. User-based testing of the AI-based prototype/system	S4. AI advisory service – Technical review of the solution S5. Testing services – testbed and use support
L4. AI-based systems are created and used in several processes and/or products of the company	Q7: AI-based systems are created and used in several processes and/or products of the company	A6. Create AI-based systems for different processes and/or products A7. Put the created AI-based systems in use	S4. AI advisory service – Technical review of the solution S5. Testing services – testbed and use support

7   Conclusions and future work

The paper presented an ongoing research project aiming to create an AI implementation capability development planning tool for SMEs (AICapDev tool) and highlighted the capability assessment part of it. The problem definition, analysis of existing AI MMs and related work, development strategy, and the core elements of AI implementation capability assessment were demonstrated.

The next steps of the current research:

- Elaborate the dependencies between capability levels and the process of selecting the most needed *next* capability levels by taking into account these dependencies and strategic importance of AI implementation capability dimensions;
- Conceptual evaluation and comparison of the AICapDev tool;

- Empirical evaluation of the AICapDev tool using pilots with SMEs;
- Update the AICapDev tool based on the feedback from the evaluation;
- Extension of the AICapDev tool with an AI skills framework to support AI skills assessment and development.

8   Acknowledgment

The research is supported by the project AI DRIVER! – Digital business transformations. Human AI interaction in service business and open education (Finnish Ministry of Education and Culture), 2021-2024.

References

1. Enholm, I.M., Papagiannidis, E., Mikalef, P. (2022) Artificial Intelligence and Business Value: a Literature Review. Inf Syst Front 24, 1709–1734.
2. Davenport, T. H., & Ronanki, R. (2018). Artificial intelligence for the real world. Harvard Business Review, 96(1), 108–116.
3. Heilala, J., Helaakoski, H., Kuivanen, R., Kääriäinen, J., & Saari, L. (2020). A review of digitalisation in the Finnish manufacturing SME companies. VTT Technical Research Centre of Finland.
4. EU recommendation 2003/361 - EU Commission Recommendation of 6 May 2003 concerning the definition of micro, small and medium-sized enterprises. URL: https://eur-lex.europa.eu/legal-content/EN/TXT/?uri=CELEX:32003H0361, last accessed 2024/11/11.
5. Moilanen, T. & Laatikainen, E. (2023). Challenges SMEs face in implementing artifical intelligence. International Journal of Advances in Electronics and Computer Science, 10(10).
6. Oldemeyer, L., Jede, A., & Teuteberg, F. (2024). Investigation of artificial intelligence in SMEs: a systematic review of the state of the art and the main implementation challenges. *Management Review Quarterly*, 1-43.
7. Czyżewska-Misztal, D. (2024). The European Union's Approach to Artificial Intelligence from a Territorial Perspective: The Case of DIHs and EDIHs Programmes. Prace Naukowe Uniwersytetu Ekonomicznego we Wrocławiu, 68(2), 1-11.
8. Saari, L., Kuusisto, O., & Pirttikangas, S. (2019). AI maturity web tool helps organisations proceed with AI. VTT Technical Research Centre of Finland. VTT White Paper URL: https://cris.vtt.fi/en/publications/ai-maturity-web-tool-helps-organisations-proceed-with-ai, last accessed 2024/11/11.
9. Sadiq, R. B., Safie, N., Abd Rahman, A. H., & Goudarzi, S. (2021). Artificial intelligence maturity model: a systematic literature review. *PeerJ Computer Science*, 7, e661.
10. Schuster, T., Waidelich, L., & Volz, R. (2021). Maturity models for the assessment of artificial intelligence in small and medium-sized enterprises. In Digital Transformation: 13th PLAIS EuroSymposium on Digital Transformation, PLAIS EuroSymposium 2021, Sopot, Poland, September 23, 2021, Proceedings 13 (pp. 22-36). Springer Publishing.
11. Sonntag, M., Mehmann, S., Mehmann, J., & Teuteberg, F. (2024). Development and Evaluation of a Maturity Model for AI Deployment Capability of Manufacturing Companies. Information Systems Management, 1-31.

12. Schuster, T., Waidelich, L. (2022). Maturity of Artificial Intelligence in SMEs: Privacy and Ethics Dimensions. In: Camarinha-Matos, L.M., Ortiz, A., Boucher, X., Osório, A.L. (eds) Collaborative Networks in Digitalization and Society 5.0. PRO-VE 2022. IFIP Advances in Information and Communication Technology, vol 662. Springer, Cham.

13. Bettoni, A., Matteri, D., Montini, E., Gładysz, B., & Carpanzano, E. (2021). An AI adoption model for SMEs: A conceptual framework. IFAC-PapersOnLine, 54(1), 702-708.

14. Bettoni, A., Corti, D., Matteri, D., Montini, E., Fiorello, M., Masiero, S.& Ejsmont, K. (2021). KITT4SME report 2021: Artificial Intelligence adoption in European Small Medium Enterprises.

15. Weber, M., Engert, M., Schaffer, N., Weking, J., & Krcmar, H. (2023). Organizational capabilities for AI implementation—coping with inscrutability and data dependency in ai. Information Systems Frontiers, 25(4), 1549-1569.

16. Mikalef, P., & Gupta, M. (2021). Artificial intelligence capability: Conceptualization, measurement calibration, and empirical study on its impact on organizational creativity and firm performance. *Information & Management, 58*(3), 103434.

17. Sjödin, D., Parida, V., Palmié, M., & Wincent, J. (2021). How AI capabilities enable business model innovation. Journal of Business Research.

18. Fukas, P., & Thomas, O. (2023). Developing a Reference Model for Artificial Intelligence Management. In ECIS 2023 Research-in-Progress Papers. 89.

19. Becker, J., Knackstedt, R., & Pöppelbuß, J. (2009). Developing maturity models for IT management: A procedure model and its application. Business & Information Systems Engineering, 1, 213-222.

20. Pöppelbuß, J., & Röglinger, M. (2011). What makes a useful maturity model? A framework of general design principles for maturity models and its demonstration in business process management.

21. Van Steenbergen, M., Bos, R., Brinkkemper, S., Van De Weerd, I., & Bekkers, W. (2010). The design of focus area maturity models. In *Global Perspectives on Design Science Research: 5th International Conference, DESRIST 2010, St. Gallen, Switzerland, June 4-5, 2010. Proceedings. 5* (pp. 317-332). Springer Berlin Heidelberg.

22. Sanchez-Puchol, F., & Pastor-Collado, J. A. (2017). Focus area maturity models: A comparative review. In Information Systems: 14th European, Mediterranean, and Middle Eastern Conference, EMCIS 2017, Coimbra, Portugal, September 7-8, 2017, Proceedings 14 (pp. 531-544). Springer International Publishing.

23. TOGAF business capability planning (TOGAF, 2023) URL: https://pubs.opengroup.org/togaf-standard/business-architecture/business-capability-planning.html, last accessed 2024/11/11.

24. Gavrilova, T., Kudryavtsev, D., & Grinberg, E. (2019). Aesthetic knowledge diagrams: bridging understanding and communication. *Knowledge Management, Arts, and Humanities: Interdisciplinary Approaches and the Benefits of Collaboration*, 97-117.

25. Ross, D. T. (1985). Applications and Extensions of SADT. *Computer, 18*(04), 25-34.

26. Kreutzer, R. T., Sirrenberg, M., Kreutzer, R. T., & Sirrenberg, M. (2020). AI challenge—how artificial intelligence can be anchored in a company. Understanding Artificial Intelligence: Fundamentals, Use Cases and Methods for a Corporate AI Journey, 235-273.

27. Burgess, A., & Burgess, A. (2018). Starting an AI journey. The Executive Guide to Artificial Intelligence: How to identify and implement applications for AI in your organization, 91-116.

Introducing AI to German SMEs – Practical Insights into Challenges and Future Research Directions

Lukas Weiss[1,2], Michael Möhring[1] and Keshav Dahal[2]

[1] AI-Lab Stuttgart for SMEs, HHZ, Reutlingen University, Reutlingen 72762, Germany
[2] University of the West of Scotland, Paisley PA1 2BE, UK
Lukas.Weiss@Reutlingen-University.DE
Michael.Moehring@Reutlingen-University.DE
Keshav.Dahal@uws.ac.uk

Abstract. Rapid changes in the business environment require adopting new technologies to maintain the pace of change and improve business results. This can be achieved through the adoption of artificial intelligence (AI). Small and medium-sized enterprises (SMEs) often face challenges regarding AI adoption. However, SMEs are often marginalized in research. For us as a regional AI lab, it is important to understand the challenges of regional SMEs to better help them adopt AI. Therefore, an expert study was conducted. Six categories of challenges were identified. The most frequently identified category was "lack of experience". The study shows practitioners need clear guidelines and a safe testing environment to implement AI projects.

Zusammenfassung. Die raschen Veränderungen im Geschäftsumfeld erfordern die Einführung neuer Technologien, um das Tempo der Veränderungen beizubehalten und die Geschäftsergebnisse zu verbessern. Dies kann durch den Einsatz von künstlicher Intelligenz (KI) erreicht werden. Kleine und mittlere Unternehmen (KMU) stehen bei der Einführung von KI oft vor Herausforderungen. Allerdings werden KMU in der Forschung oft an den Rand gedrängt. Für uns als regionales KI-Labor ist es wichtig, die Herausforderungen der regionalen KMUs zu verstehen, um sie bei der Einführung von KI besser unterstützen zu können. Deshalb wurde eine Expertenstudie durchgeführt. Es wurden sechs Kategorien von Herausforderungen ermittelt, die häufigste Kategorie war „Mangel an Erfahrung". Die Studie zeigt, dass Praktiker klare Richtlinien und eine sichere Testumgebung benötigen, um KI-Projekte umzusetzen.

Keywords: SME, AI Adoption, Challenges, Expert Study

M. Möhring et al. (Hrsg.), *Herman Hollerith Conference 2024*, Informatik aktuell,
https://doi.org/10.1007/978-3-658-48215-2_4

1   Introduction

A rapidly changing technological environment dominates the present economy [1]. In addition, the speed of adoption of new technologies (e.g., artificial intelligence (AI)) has increased [2]. Also, the recent COVID pandemic has increased the speed of adoption of digital technologies overall [3], especially for SMEs in Europe, where the adoption of digital technologies leads to improved business outcomes [4]. The integration of technologies, specifically AI, into existing organizations can improve business outcomes [5], lead to a significant improvement in various departments in companies (e.g., marketing departments) [6], and can lead to strategic and economic advantage [6], [7]. To achieve these benefits, the technology should be adopted quickly in this volatile environment [8]. The problem here is that the use of digital technologies and, thus, AI brings with it many opportunities but also challenges [9] that need to be understood and overcome [10].

A recent survey by Fraunhofer [8] found that 84% of the larger companies in Germany are working with AI—15 % more than small and medium-sized enterprises (SMEs). In line with this, another study shows a 10% lower AI adoption rate of SMEs than large companies [11]. However, SMEs are the majority of companies in the European Union [12] and should adopt AI to stay competitive. Most current research addresses the AI adoption of medium-sized to large enterprises and organizations (e.g., [13], [14], [15], [16]). The results are not transferable to SMEs in general due to the individual specifics of small enterprises [13]. This is also supported by the insights of our regional AI lab in Germany, where we supported more than 40 SMEs in adopting AI technology. This interesting line of research has not yet been fully explored from a practical and research-oriented point of view. Therefore, we started a regional AI lab to support SMEs. It is important to find out what challenges regional SMEs face when adopting AI to define actions to improve the adoption rate and derive implications for new lines of research. Therefore, within this paper, we want to show current practical empirical insights from practice and show impacts based on the following research question: RQ: "What challenges do SMEs in Germany encounter when introducing AI technologies into the organization?"

The present research follows a specific structure to answer the research question. Firstly, the section on background emphasizes the lack of research into the challenges SMEs face with AI adoption. This is followed by a detailed description of the data collection process, analysis methods employed in the research, and a brief outline of the sample characteristics. Subsequently, the results section presents the research's findings. Finally, the concluding section summarizes and discusses the results, considering the research's objectives and suggesting avenues for further research.

2   Background

According to the currently published empirical findings based on Webster and Watson [17], there is sparse research on AI Adoption [13], [14], [15], [16] in SMEs. In the available sources, most of the results were generated by data from medium-sized to large companies. The research results are still in their early stages. They are seen as opening up the research path in this area, initially checking the compatibility of grounded theories with AI adoption [14], thereby not addressing the challenges that real companies often face when introducing AI technology. Further research is also required to better understand the impact of AI adoption in practice and develop guidelines for the improved adoption of AI technology [13]. Practical insights enable this. These surveys identified potential reasons for the low adoption rate of AI technologies in German SMEs. For instance, one study found that the required data may not be available in the format necessary for direct use in AI applications [18]. While another study found that data availability may not be the primary bottleneck for SMEs, data quality and preparation could be [19]. Another study already presents a potential solution for data challenges, but it is designed for larger companies and is not practical for SMEs [20]. As many SMEs have challenges while adopting AI technologies [18] and using them [11], [21], even though the adoption of AI technology can give SMEs an economic advantage [12], it is promising to investigate this area further [22]. Due to the adaptation of the EU AI Act, there will be further implications regarding this regulation for companies within the EU in the future [23]. The potential problems identified are empirically based mainly on data from large and medium-sized companies and are therefore not specifically empirically focused on our gap for SMEs. Considering that many SMEs struggle with both the adoption and utilization of AI technologies [18], [11], [21], it is promising and essential to conduct further research in this area to gain deeper insights and enable smoother integration of AI [22].

3   First Insights into Challenges for SMEs

As a regional AI lab, we provide SMEs with easy access to AI advice, ranging from initial consultation to pilot support. We have noticed that the companies we support often face problems and challenges that have not been addressed so far in detail in research [24]. The paper is an initial place to discuss it with the community and strengthen activities in this important research area for practice and research. To systematically identify these challenges for SMEs and use the newly gained insights to support the companies better, we conducted a qualitative expert study to understand better the challenges SMEs face at a regional level.

3.1   Research Method and Data Collection

We conducted a qualitative expert study during an industry forum at a regional AI Lab for SMEs in Germany in the fourth quarter of 2023. Qualitative research approaches are a good starting point for fields that have not yet been fully explored [25], [26] and generate first insights and a foundation for hypotheses. The participants were split randomly into three independent groups by the researcher and conducted a group discussion on challenges with AI. The total duration of the discussion was approx. 60 minutes. A sufficient sample (as recommended by other researchers [27], [28]) of n=15 industry experts from different industry sectors, as shown in Table 1, took part in the study.

Table 1. Expert Industry Sectors and Roles

Participants	Industry	Participants	Role
n = 6	Consulting	n = 8	Managing Director
n = 2	Media agency	n = 1	Business Operations Partner
n = 1	Food & Beverage	n = 1	Senior Data Consultant
n = 1	Wholesale	n = 1	Sales Manager
n = 1	AI Startup	n = 1	Digitalization Manager
n = 1	Non-profit organization	n = 1	Principal
n = 1	Smart home	n = 1	Innovation manager
n = 1	Education	n = 1	Volunteer
n = 1	IT	-	-
Total: n = 15		Total: n = 15	

The industry sector "Consulting" was combined and is listed in Table 1. It has the following subcategories: business-, data-, management-, and tax-consulting. The participants have not yet implemented AI technologies in their company's operations. This must be ensured to answer the question without bias. Participants with various roles (Table 1) participated in the study to improve the quality and obtain results from different perspectives.

We used two coding cycles to extract the main themes from the results. The first coding cycle consisted of descriptive coding [29]. This was performed to gain insights into the data and its descriptive information. Codes were extracted from the individual discussions during the expert study. In a second cycle, the previously created codes were merged into a smaller number of pattern codes. Pattern coding was used [29] to extract the expert study's main themes and aspects, key ideas, and concepts. By discussing and assessing the coding process with a group of three researchers and students, an evaluation of the researchers helped to ensure validity and reliability.

3.2   Results

After data analysis through coding, six categories of challenges for SMEs were identified (as shown in Table 2). It is important to emphasize that this represents the problems of the study participants at an abstract level; therefore, these are explained in more detail below, and implications are made based on individual findings.

Table 2. Challenges

Frequency	Challenges
n = 7	Experience
n = 5	Economic resources
n = 4	Plug-and-play solution
n = 4	Data problem
n = 3	Area of application
n = 3	Data protection
Total: n = 27	

Experience

Experiences are to determine what has happened, differences, and similarities, and to build up knowledge [30]. This category covers a wide range of problems and challenges the study participants face. This includes the participants' general lack of experience in artificial intelligence and specific areas of AI, such as understanding the principles of natural language processing. In addition, the participants have problems understanding and interpreting the predictions of machine learning algorithms. Understanding why and how predictions are made is fundamental to accepting and building trust for an AI model's decision [31]. This is particularly true when more complex systems are used, and the processing is not easy to comprehend.

Economic resources

Economic resources are the inputs for production processes, such as land, labor force, or capital [32]. Participants report that human and monetary resources are essential. These two types of resources are generally only available to a limited extent among the participants companies in the study, as they have few financial resources for (initially) unprofitable projects within the SME sector. Reallocating already limited human resources to new projects and core activities is also challenging. A quick win is, therefore, of the highest importance for such projects. Moreover, participants reported that investment certainty for projects involving AI technologies is non-transparent, making it challenging to allocate resources.

Plug-and-play solution

A plug-and-play solution is a product that can provide a solution to an existing problem without customization to the existing environment [33]. This category emphasizes the difficulty of finding a pre-existing toolkit for use. Furthermore, study participants encounter the challenge of no off-the-shelf solution in AI, particularly in machine learning, as most applications must be tailored to the specific use case since careful data preparation is needed [34]. Participants reported that they did not have an overview of the possibilities of AI at the beginning of their AI journey. They also report that they cannot find pre-made solutions for domain-specific problems.

Data problem

A data problem includes the lack of necessary high-quality data and finding the proper application for the data [18]. It is described that there are data silos, but it is not clear what the data could be used for. The challenge of the right data quality is also discussed. Another challenge mentioned is the data culture in the companies, which is about the awareness of the company and its employees for handling data in general. Another challenge is non-existent or too little data. This challenge is often faced within projects related to data [35].

Area of application

This category described the concerns about finding a meaningful use of AI technologies, which is often lacking [18]. In particular, the challenge is to find a suitable application for AI models that handle text. The participants report the challenges of assigning a suitable business case with the correct available data (types) to the suitable AI algorithm and thus finding the proper use case. This is a critical challenge as AI technology solutions are needed to enhance business value [5].

Data protection

Data protection means ethical and legal aspects as well as user trust [36]. In this category, the focus group discusses challenges relating to the data protection of AI technology and the associated solutions. It is essential to the respondents that the data are secure at all times and not passed on to third parties. Another challenge discussed is ensuring the data ownership remains with the respective company. Another challenge the participants face about data protection is that this topic is very complicated, and there are no simple solutions. They state that legal advisors usually have to be consulted for support.

4   Conclusion, Discussion, and Future Directions

The rapidly changing and volatile business environment efforts the adoption of technology [1]. Adopting technology, especially AI technology, also enhances the business outcome [5]; overcoming the barriers to introducing AI technology is essential. The first step is understanding the challenges SMEs in Germany face while introducing AI technology. Research in AI adoption for European SMEs is a field that has not yet been widely explored. Mid-size to large-sized companies have a totally different environment and resources [37]. From a practical point of view, the paper described the insights into the challenges collected from an expert study running at an AI lab in South Germany within this important research area. Six different categories of challenges answered the proposed research question. The challenges found should be further investigated and discussed. The most prevalent issues included limited resources, difficulties using existing tools (plug-and-play solution), data issues, unspecific application areas, and data protection. The study demonstrates that these challenges impact the implementation of AI in smaller enterprises. Big enterprises have different challenges, such as competitive pressure, compliance with industry-specific standards [13], or managerial obstacles [14]. However, without addressing this important sector in AI adoption, we will lose a lot of competitiveness and research insights.

The small, regionally-focused sample (n=15) of German SMEs limits the ability to generalize findings to a broader population of SMEs in general, even within Germany, as the challenges encountered may vary across different sectors, regions, and scales of operation. This highlights the urgent need to address these limitations, as they could significantly impact the understanding and implementation of AI in SMEs. Additionally, relying on qualitative data from a single forum and subjective expert opinions may introduce bias[25], as these perspectives do not quantitatively assess the scale or impact of each identified challenge, potentially omitting other significant factors in AI adoption. Another limitation of this study is that it is based on the frequency of challenges in the sample rather than a structured ranking of their relative importance. Future research could enhance these findings by employing methods such as the Delphi technique, allowing for expert-driven prioritization and providing a more precise hierarchy of challenges based on their perceived impact and urgency.

This research extends the existing research on AI adoption and the challenges SMEs face in Europe, especially in Germany, in introducing AI technology projects (e.g., [24],[38],[37]) and opens new ways for discussing solutions and research approaches for adopting AI in this field for SMEs. Practitioners can use this to understand better the challenges faced when implementing AI projects in smaller companies. In this way, organizations can prepare for these challenges before AI projects and thus achieve a higher success rate in realizing such projects. The successful implementation of AI projects makes SMEs more competitive and increases the outcome [5]. Since this study was limited to German SMEs, due to the research method, the sample is limited and should be supported by quantitative methods in further research.

Further research and discussions could build upon the results of this work to gain a deeper understanding of the factors influencing AI's introduction and the possibilities of overcoming these challenges for SMEs. We will use crowdsourcing tools to collect and review together the preliminary insights and link this to an important topic in an early stage.

References

1.   P. C. Verhoef et al., Digital transformation: A multidisciplinary reflection and research agenda, J. Bus. Res., vol. 122, pp. 889–901, Jan. 2021, doi: 10.1016/j.jbusres.2019.09.022.

2.   M. Cosa, Business Digital Transformation: Strategy Adaptation, Communication and Future Agenda, J. Strategy Manag., vol. 17, no. 2, pp. 244–259, May 2024, doi: 10.1108/JSMA-09-2023-0233.

3.   K. Li, D. J. Kim, K. R. Lang, R. J. Kauffman, and M. Naldi, How should we understand the digital economy in Asia? Critical assessment and research agenda, Electron. Commer. R. A., vol. 44, p. 101004, Nov. 2020, doi: 10.1016/j.elerap.2020.101004.

4.   M. Skare, M. De Las Mercedes De Obesso, and S. Ribeiro-Navarrete, Digital transformation and European small and medium enterprises (SMEs): A comparative study using digital economy and society index data, Int. J. Inf. Manage., vol. 68, p. 102594, Feb. 2023, doi: 10.1016/j.ijinfomgt.2022.102594.

5.   H. Li, X. Wang, Y. Feng, Y. Qi, and J. Tian, Integration Methods and Advantages of Machine Learning with Cloud Data Warehouses, Int. J. Comput. Sci. Inf. Technol., vol. 2, no. 1, pp. 348–358, Mar. 2024, doi: 10.62051/ijcsit.v2n1.36.

6.   J. Furman and R. Seamans, AI and the Economy, Innov. Policy Econ., vol. 19, pp. 161–191, Jan. 2019, doi: 10.1086/699936.

7.   C. Hahn, T. Traunecker, M. Niever, and G. N. Basedow, Exploring AI-Driven Business Models: Conceptualization and Expectations in the Machinery Industry, in 2020 IEEE International Conference on Industrial Engineering and Engineering Management (IEEM), Singapore, Singapore: IEEE, Dec. 2020, pp. 567–570. doi: 10.1109/IEEM45057.2020.9309824.

8.   S. S. Abed, A literature review exploring the role of technology in business survival during the Covid-19 lockdowns, Int. J. Organ. Anal., vol. 30, no. 5, pp. 1045–1062, Nov. 2022, doi: 10.1108/IJOA-11-2020-2501.

9.   M. Schmidt, Einsatz von künstlicher Intelligenz für sachbearbeitende Tätigkeiten im öffentlichen Dienst, Wirtsch. Manag., vol. 16, no. 2, pp. 123–132, Apr. 2024, doi: 10.1365/s35764-024-00516-3.

10.   B. Keller, M. Möhring, and F. Augenstein, Data Analytics as a Service – Challenges and Opportunities: An Introduction to DAS-24, in INFORMATIK 2024, Bonn: Gesellschaft für Informatik e.V., 2024, pp. 1481–1489. doi: 10.18420/inf2024_128.

11.   I. Seifert et al., BMWK - Bundesministerium für Wirtschaft und Klimaschutz. Accessed: Feb.   05,   2024.   [Online].   Available: https://www.bmwk.de/Redaktion/DE/Publikationen/Studien/potenziale-kuenstlichen-intelligenz-im-produzierenden-gewerbe-in-deutsch-land.pdf?__blob=publicationFile&v=8

12.   European Commission, "SME Annual Report 2020–2021." 2021. [Online]. Available: https://ec.europa.eu/docsroom/documents/46062

13.   L. Pumplun, C. Tauchert, and M. Heidt, A New Organizational Chassis for Artificial Intelligence - Exploring Organizational Readiness Factors, in European Conference on Information Systems, 2019.

14.   S. Alsheibani, C. Messom, and Y. Cheung, Re-thinking the Competitive Landscape of Artificial Intelligence, presented at the Hawaii International Conference on System Sciences, 2020. doi: 10.24251/HICSS.2020.718.

15.   S. Chatterjee, N. P. Rana, Y. K. Dwivedi, and A. M. Baabdullah, Understanding AI adoption in manufacturing and production firms using an integrated TAM-TOE

model, Technol. Forecast. Soc., vol. 170, p. 120880, Sep. 2021, doi: 10.1016/j.techfore.2021.120880.

16.   H. Chen, L. Li, and Y. Chen, Explore success factors that impact artificial intelligence adoption on telecom industry in China, J. Manag. Anal., vol. 8, no. 1, pp. 36–68, Jan. 2021, doi: 10.1080/23270012.2020.1852895.

17.   J. Webster and R. T. Watson, Analyzing the past to prepare for the future: Writing a literature review, Mis Quart., pp. xiii–xxiii, 2002.

18.   C. Dukino et al., Künstliche Intelligenz in der Unternehmenspraxis, 2019, doi: 10.24406/PUBLICA-FHG-300040.

19.   B. T. Hazen, C. A. Boone, J. D. Ezell, and L. A. Jones-Farmer, Data quality for data science, predictive analytics, and big data in supply chain management: An introduction to the problem and suggestions for research and applications, Int. J. Prod. Econ., vol. 154, pp. 72–80, Aug. 2014, doi: 10.1016/j.ijpe.2014.04.018.

20.   C. Gröger, There is no AI without data, Commun. ACM, vol. 64, no. 11, pp. 98–108, Nov. 2021, doi: 10.1145/3448247.

21.   V. Zimmermann, Artificial intelligence: high growth potential but low penetration in SMEs. [Online]. Available: https://www.kfw.de/PDF/Download-Center/Konzernthemen/Research/PDF-Dokumente-Fokus-Volkswirtschaft/Fokus-englische-Dateien/Fokus-2021-EN/Focus-No.-318-Febuary-2021-AI.pdf

22.   A. Bunte, F. Richter, and R. Diovisalvi, Why It is Hard to Find AI in SMEs: A Survey from the Practice and How to Promote It:, in Proceedings of the 13th International Conference on Agents and Artificial Intelligence, SCITEPRESS - Science and Technology Publications, 2021, pp. 614–620. doi: 10.5220/0010204106140620.

23.   Q. Ren and J. Du, Harmonizing innovation and regulation: The EU Artificial Intelligence Act in the international trade context, Comput. Law Secur. Rev., vol. 54, p. 106028, Sep. 2024, doi: 10.1016/j.clsr.2024.106028.

24.   J. Radhakrishnan, S. Gupta, and S. Prashar, Understanding Organizations' Artificial Intelligence Journey: A Qualitative Approach, Pac. Asia J. Assoc. Inf. Syst., vol. 14, pp. 43–77, Jan. 2022, doi: 10.17705/1pais.14602.

25.   J. Recker, Scientific Research in Information Systems: A Beginner's Guide. in Progress in IS. Cham: Springer International Publishing, 2021. doi: 10.1007/978-3-030-85436-2.

26.   M. Myers and D. Avison, Qualitative Research in Information Systems. 1 Oliver's Yard, 55 City Road, London England EC1Y 1SP United Kingdom: SAGE Publications, Ltd, 2002. doi: 10.4135/9781849209687.

27.   S. E. Baker, R. Edwards, and M. Doidge, How many qualitative interviews is enough?: expert voices and early career reflections on sampling and cases in qualitative research, National Centre for Research Methods, Southampton, WorkingPaper, Mar. 2012.

28.   G. Guest, A. Bunce, and L. Johnson, How Many Interviews Are Enough? An Experiment with Data Saturation and Variability, Field Method., vol. 18, no. 1, pp. 59–82, Feb. 2006, doi: 10.1177/1525822X05279903.

29.   P. Mayring, Qualitative content analysis, companion qual. res., vol. 1, no. 2, pp. 159–176, 2004.

30. K. Fox, Rethinking Experience: What Do We Mean by This Word 'Experience'?, J. Exp. Educ., vol. 31, no. 1, pp. 36–54, Aug. 2008, doi: 10.1177/105382590803100105.

31. D. Doran, S. Schulz, and T. R. Besold, What Does Explainable AI Really Mean? A New Conceptualization of Perspectives, 2017, doi: 10.48550/ARXIV.1710.00794.

32. R. M. Grant, The Resource-Based Theory of Competitive Advantage: Implications for Strategy Formulation, Calif. Manage. Rev., vol. 33, no. 3, pp. 114–135, Apr. 1991, doi: 10.2307/41166664.

33. I. A. Ridhawi, S. Otoum, M. Aloqaily, and A. Boukerche, Generalizing AI: Challenges and Opportunities for Plug and Play AI Solutions, IEEE Netw., vol. 35, no. 1, pp. 372–379, Jan. 2021, doi: 10.1109/MNET.011.2000371.

34. N. R. Njeri, Data Preparation For Machine Learning Modelling, Int. J. Comput. Appl. Technol. Res., vol. 11, no. 06, pp. 231–235, Jun. 2022, doi: 10.7753/IJCATR1106.1008.

35. F. Caputo, B. Keller, M. Möhring, L. Carrubbo, and R. Schmidt, Advancing beyond technicism when managing big data in companies' decision-making, J. Knowl. Manag., vol. 27, no. 10, pp. 2797–2809, Nov. 2023, doi: 10.1108/JKM-10-2022-0794.

36. S. Glorin, Privacy and Data Protection in ChatGPT and Other AI Chatbots: Strategies for Securing User Information, Int. J. Secur. Priv. Pervasive Comput., vol. 15, no. 1, pp. 1–14, Jul. 2023, doi: 10.4018/IJSPPC.325475.

37. M. I. Merhi, An evaluation of the critical success factors impacting artificial intelligence implementation, Int. J. Inf. Manage., vol. 69, p. 102545, Apr. 2023, doi: 10.1016/j.ijinfomgt.2022.102545.

38. A. Polisetty, D. Chakraborty, S. G, A. K. Kar, and S. Pahari, What Determines AI Adoption in Companies? Mixed-Method Evidence, J. Comput. Inform. Syst., vol. 64, no. 3, pp. 370–387, May 2024, doi: 10.1080/08874417.2023.2219668.

Realization of a Digital Product Passport for a Cross-Company Carbon Accounting

Dimitri Petrik[1][0000-0002-0244-1235], Florian Härer[2][0000-0002-2719-5368], and Felix Schöllkopf[2]

[1] Graduate School of Excellence Advanced Manufacturing Engineering (GSaME), University of Stuttgart, Nobelstr. 12, 70569 Stuttgart, Germany
dimitri.petrik@gsame.uni-stuttgart.de
[2] Klingele Paper & Packaging, Alfred-Klingele-Str. 56–76, 73630 Remshalden, Germany
{florian.haerer;felix.schoellkopf}@klingele.com

Abstract.
Achieving accurate carbon accounting across the supply chain in the packaging industry is hampered by data silos and limited automation. This paper presents an innovative approach to carbon accounting that integrates Digital Product Passports for data exchange across the entire value chain. Using the corrugated cardboard industry as a case study, it demonstrates how a DPP can serve as a central data hub to accurately calculate the product carbon footprints in accordance with Scope 3 requirements that include a whole value chain. The DPP enhances data quality by addressing gaps in carbon accounting through the involvement of all value chain actors. Additionally, the DPP supports companies in meeting regulatory requirements, such as the corporate sustainability reporting directive, while providing transparency regarding the calculation logic. The results highlight the importance of enterprise software in the realization of DPPs and show that secure and sovereign data exchange and the integration of technologies such as the Asset Administration Shell and the Eclipse Dataspace Connector are beneficial for the integration of process data into a DPP.

Zusammenfassung. Eine exakte Ermittlung und Bilanzierung von CO_2-Emissionen entlang der gesamten Lieferkette in der Verpackungsindustrie wird durch Datensilos und eine begrenzte Automatisierung erschwert. In diesem Artikel wird ein innovativer Ansatz zur CO_2-Bilanzierung vorgestellt, der Digitale Produktpässe (DPP) für die Datenteilung über die gesamte Wertschöpfungskette hinweg integriert. Am Beispiel der Wellpappenindustrie wird demonstriert, wie ein DPP als zentraler Data Hub dienen kann, um den CO_2-Fußabdruck von Produkten in Übereinstimmung mit den Scope-3-Anforderungen, die die gesamte Wertschöpfungskette umfassen, genau zu berechnen. Der DPP steigert die Datenqualität, indem er Lücken in der CO_2-Bilanzierung durch die Einbindung aller Akteure in der Wertschöpfungskette schließt.

Darüber hinaus unterstützt der DPP Unternehmen dabei, regulatorische Anforderungen wie die Corporate Sustainability Reporting Directive zuerfüllen und bietet gleichzeitig Transparenz über die Berechnungslogik. Die Ergebnisse verdeutlichen die zentrale Bedeutung von Enterprise Software für die Realisierung von DPPs und zeigen, dass ein sicherer und souveräner Datenaustausch sowie die Einbindung von Technologien wie der Asset Administration Shell und dem Eclipse Dataspace Connector für die Integration von Prozessdaten in einen DPP von Vorteil sind.

Keywords: Carbon accounting, CO2 accounting, Scope 3, Digital Product Passport, data space, digital sustainability.

1   Introduction

Given the major challenges of our time, such as climate change and resource crises, industrial organizations must perform sustainably [1, 2]. The European Union is intensifying its efforts to reduce carbon emissions in all sectors of the economy, including industry. To date, organizational carbon emissions are classified into three so-called scopes, which greatly differ in their complexity concerning complexity and reporting [4]. Under the international Greenhouse Gas Protocol, greenhouse gas accounting currently focuses primarily on Scope 1 and Scope 2 [5]. Scope 1 emissions include direct emissions from sources that are owned or controlled by the company, such as the on-site burning of fossil fuels in company facilities or company-owned vehicles [5]. Scope 2 emissions are indirect emissions from the generation of purchased electricity, steam, heating, and cooling consumed by the reporting company, essentially representing "imported" emissions [5].
While Scope 1 and Scope 2 emissions are mandatory to report, Scope 3 emissions accounting has thus far been optional. Scope 3 emissions include all other indirect emissions that occur within a company's value chain, both upstream and downstream (e.g., goods and services, transportation, or product portfolio) [6, 7]. Scope 3 emissions are particularly significant because they often represent the largest portion of a company's total greenhouse gas footprint, frequently amounting to as much as four times a company's own direct operational emissions [8]. Considering the expectation that Scope 3 will become mandatory, holistic carbon accounting along the entire value chain could make both regulatory and economic sense for companies.

Companies follow the *Greenhouse Gas (GHG) Protocol* frameworks [9]. Thinking beyond the legal requirements, a carbon accounting approach that spans the entire supply chain could enable the identification and elimination of inefficiencies and causes of emissions in the supply chain, strengthening companies' resilience and competitiveness [10]. However, such endeavors are highly dependent on the quality of data, which requires reliable data and extensive analyses [11].

Software and digital technologies are expected to aid organizations in collecting and analyzing sustainability data [12]. Technologies such as the *Asset Administration Shell (AAS)*, the *Eclipse Dataspace Connector (EDC)*, and the *OPC Unified*

Architecture (OPC UA) protocol provide a suitable basis for the efficient collection of data [13] since industrial organizations are usually integrated into value chains. Despite increasing initiatives and recognition of the innovative and transformative potential of data, organizations face a variety of technical and business barriers that hinder the shared use of data across the enterprise [14, 15]. Collecting relevant production and logistics data is challenging, as many companies use heterogeneous landscapes from operational information systems. Therefore, integrating *Enterprise Resource Planning (ERP) systems*, *Manufacturing Execution Systems (MES)*, and logistics software systems is necessary to make this data available for cross-company carbon balancing [16].

However, a lot of data remains in silos, which hampers cross-company exchange [15, 17]. Furthermore, sustainability data collection is not automated in many organizations and occurs on a project-by-project basis. Such a state of sustainability management is inefficient and error-prone. A cross-company, automated solution that is accepted by all partners in the value chain could significantly improve the quality of carbon accounting [18, 19]. An important prerequisite for this is enabled by the establishment of data spaces, such as Catena-X for the automotive supply chain [20]. However, data spaces also face various challenges when it comes to data sharing, especially poor interoperability and availability of data [14]. To address the challenges of data spaces and the persisting inaccuracies in carbon accounting, a *Digital Product Passport (DPP)* is considered a viable solution that can be set up inter-organizationally in a data space [21, 22]. Until now, DPPs have been primarily associated with the legal requirements resulting from the Ecodesign for Sustainable Products Regulation (ESPR), which entered into force on the 18th of July 2024 [23]. However, a DPP is expected to unlock further benefits and to be used to improve carbon accounting. Hence, this paper reports the learnings from a case study within the packaging industry, proposing a carbon accounting approach, which integrates a DPP.

The structure of this paper is as follows: The next section reviews relevant literature on sustainable development, the EU's legislative framework, and data-sharing approaches such as data spaces and DPP. A narrative review was performed to present the related work, combining initial informal searches with more systematic database level searches. This approach ensured both a broad exploration of the DPP research stream at the outset and a focused identification of relevant sources based on an inductive content analysis [24, 25]. Section 3 outlines the methodology, detailing the case study approach with PackCorp in the corrugated cardboard industry. Section 4 presents the case study results, illustrating current practices in carbon accounting and proposing a DPP-enhanced approach. Finally, Section 5 discusses the limitations, and future research directions for scaling the DPP-based carbon accounting framework.

2   Related Work

The current idea of sustainable development comprises three central dimensions: economic, ecological, and social aspects. These must be considered and integrated together, as they are closely interlinked and influence each other. This understanding forms the basis of the three-pillar sustainability model [26]. Various initiatives have been launched, such as the ESPR or the *Corporate Sustainability Reporting Directive* (CSRD). These EU directives extend the Non-Financial Reporting Directive and oblige companies to prepare more comprehensive sustainability reports. The reports draw on calculations defined by the methodologies, such as the *life cycle assessment (LCA)*, incorporating all inputs and outputs for value-added processes relevant to resource consumption. To get a holistic picture, which could eventually lead to efficiency gains in economic and ecological performance, carbon accounting should cover the entire supply chain. To access the data outside the company boundaries, institutionalized approaches such as data spaces are purposeful.

Data spaces are understood as inter-organizational information systems that enable data-sharing scenarios across organizational boundaries through mechanisms that ensure secure and trustworthy data sharing [27, 28]. Data spaces establish specific common agreements, rules, and standards that can help different organizations from a supply chain to share data. The most prominent implementation of a technical standard is the EDC, which can be adopted by the organizations of a data space for peer-to-peer data transfer. It can further regulate data access and usage control, acting as a trusted environment [29].

While a connector can reduce the interoperability effort, it is not the solution to the problem of data models, which can be heterogeneous in a supply chain. To address this problem, DPPs seem to provide a purposeful solution. Among the diverse definitions of a DPP, the European Commission defines it as a *"product-specific data set, which can be electronically accessed through a data carrier to electronically register, process and share product-related information amongst supply chain businesses, authorities and consumers"* [30].

As part of the aforementioned ESPR, DPPs are becoming mandatory for new products in some industries, such as batteries or tires, to create transparency over material use. This is expected to enable the circular economy, as different stakeholders can be informed about the composition of products at the material level, the product history (damage effects relevant to the materials and their value), or disassembly options via the DPP [31]. However, as current studies show, a DPP can also make sense for tangibles in industries where the DPP is not mandatory [32]. A DPP can serve as a single point of truth and form a data model accepted by all actors in a data space, which contains information at the granularity of individual products or batches. The data stored in a DPP can be made accessible to the end customers and to the actors in the supply chain through digital and physical interfaces [30]. In addition, Jensen and colleagues [29] emphasize that a DPP acts as an information system throughout the entire product lifecycle, integrating different categories of data that capture product-specific details from design to end-of-life. They suggest that the DPP accumulates data from all phases of the product lifecycle: Design, production, usage, and disposal, requiring all stakeholders in the value chain to collaborate and ensure data transparency and accessibility. By integrating diverse data categories [33], summarized in Tab. 1, the DPP enhances decision-making related to the sustainability management, which incorporates circular strategies and carbon accounting.

Table 1. Data categories based on [33].

Data Category	Description
Utilization and Maintenance	Information about the environment in which the product was located at the time of use. This also includes the service log and the repair history.
Product Identification	Information to uniquely identify a product (e.g., serial numbers, model numbers, manufacturing data and country of origin).
Products and Materials	Information on the availability of spare parts or a list of hazardous substances.
Guidelines and Instructions	Descriptive information about the product, such as a service manual for non-destructive disassembly, installation or maintenance.
Supply Chain and Reverse Logistics	Information about the life cycle of a product, including suppliers, logistics, take-back, and recycling processes.
Environmental Data	Information about the environmental impact of a product and the environmental conditions under which the product was operated (e.g., the environmental footprint).
Compliance	Information on compliance with product-relevant legal regulations, standards, and guidelines.

Various internal data, for instance from digital twins [34], can also be integrated into a DPP. However, digital twins and DPPs are two different notions. As shown in Figure 1, the data use cascades between an internal and external use, whereby the inter-organizational use of DPPs can be supported by the connectivity standards provided by data spaces [27, 33, 34]. As one can see from the environmental data category in Table 1, DPP data can be meaningfully used for carbon accounting for specific domains, as explained in the next section. Using the packaging industry as an exemplary setting, the following case study explains the current state and how it can be achieved in line with the presented objectives.

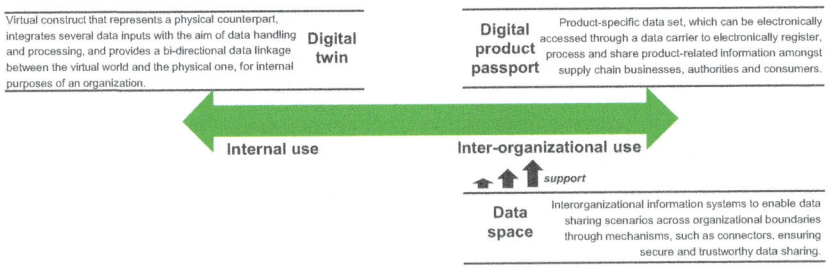

Fig. 1. Cascading of data use between a data space, a digital twin, and a digital product passport

3   Methodology

The results of this study were obtained in a collaborative project with practitioners and, therefore, have the character of a case study. The setting of the case study is the corrugated cardboard industry for packaging. As a material, corrugated cardboard is a fully recyclable and biodegradable packaging material. In Germany, for instance, corrugated cardboard packaging is almost completely recycled, and the value chain for corrugated cardboard already forms a "closed loop". Therefore, corrugated cardboard competes with plastic packaging. Customers, e.g., in retail, increasingly want to know the sustainability performance in order to make an informed decision about the packaging of their own products. As a result, it is crucial for the corrugated cardboard industry for packaging to perform carbon accounting precisely.

The case firm *Klingele Paper and Packaging Group (PackCorp)* is one of Germany's largest corrugated base paper and corrugated board packaging manufacturers. Their plants employ 3,200 people and generated combined sales of 1.3 billion EUR in 2023. The product range of the case study partner comprises corrugated base papers based on recovered paper and sustainable virgin fiber, corrugated sheet boards, and innovative and sustainable packaging solutions (mainly made of corrugated cardboard) for numerous industries and applications. PackCorp is already using up to 90 percent recycled paper to produce corrugated board packaging. PackCorp can be considered an industry incumbent firm and a dominant actor in its value chain. Therefore, to advance the carbon accounting toward Scope 3 coverage, PackCorp occupies a beneficial position in the value chain to drive sustainability actions such as Scope 3 accounting throughout its entire supply chain. This goal necessitates the creation of an inter-organizational information system (i.e., a data space), which can use a concept like a DPP for gathering and distributing data relevant to carbon accounting.

To achieve the research objective and gain a better understanding of the stakeholders in the supply chain, a survey was conducted among 36 partners and key customers of PackCorp. This survey aimed to identify the specific challenges and expectations of the partners regarding sustainable business practices and carbon accounting. The survey was carried out using a combination of qualitative and quantitative interview questions and was analyzed through content analysis. One of the key findings confirmed the need for reliable carbon data with the consensus of the supply chain actors on a certain goal: Achieving carbon neutrality across the entire value chain, and the importance of closed-loop systems. The survey participants also expressed their willingness to collaborate with PackCorp on future digital solutions for sustainability to meet these expectations: "*We trust (PackCorp) when it comes to digital services in the area of sustainability*". The reason for this stems from the increasing requirements from customers and investors of PackCorp's partners in the value chain: "*Our internal and external stakeholders expect us to find solutions for various sustainability issues*". These statements highlight the need for transparency and information exchange relevant to carbon accounting throughout the value chain, enabling Scope 3 reporting [35, 36]. Furthermore, the survey results served as a foundation for in-depth discussions with PackCorp's experts on the design of a collaborative digital service in the area of sustainability and laid the groundwork for achieving the research objective.

When incomplete knowledge is present for the development of artifacts and practitioners are to be supported, a collaborative approach is appropriate to address this need together with experts from the field and facilitate the necessary transfer of knowledge between academia and practice [37]. Various instruments can be used to collaborate with experts on a solution [38, 39]. The moderation method is best suited to reflect on the input from the previously conducted survey with practitioners and supports the subsequent concept development, as it allows for flexible and structured collaboration with a group of practitioners. Hence, the author team utilized moderation techniques to integrate all participating experts equally, facilitate collaborative ideation processes, and create consensus on a solution. Additionally, techniques for illustration and visualization were used. Therefore, a focus group workshop was performed for this study.

The workshop group consisted of six experts representing various key departments of PackCorp, including pre-development, product development, sustainability management, innovation management, energy management and IT. These diverse perspectives within the collaborative approach were crucial for identifying potential solutions for the development and implementation of a DPP to enhance carbon accounting. This allowed for the different perspectives on data integration and provision for an enhanced carbon accounting, which integrates the entire value chain. The results of the previously conducted survey also provided important insights by highlighting the urgent need for transparency and reliable carbon data. Therefore, it was particularly important to integrate data sources from different company departments to improve the accuracy of carbon accounting while breaking down existing data silos. A qualitative group survey was also performed during the focus group to gather in-depth information on the technical and organizational requirements for implementing a DPP, particularly with regard to its integration into existing enterprise software landscape.

During the research workshop, the researchers took on the role of moderators and guided the discussions. During the collaborative analysis and solution phase the researchers ensured that currently perceived limitations of the carbon accounting are addressed by the intended solution. All the responses were recorded, transcribed, and subsequently analyzed using inductive content analysis to support the achievement of the research goal. The workshop process began with an analysis of the current state of carbon accounting. To achieve this, the types of data used for the already implemented carbon accounting were identified, using the example of a specific *product carbon footprint (PCF)*, along with the data sources (i.e., the systems where the data is stored) and the data provision process. In addition, PackCorp's software landscape was analyzed to understand which systems allow bidirectional data exchange with a DPP. Insights from the aforementioned survey with PackCorp's supply chain were also visually incorporated at this stage. In the solution phase, Götz's framework for a DPP [30] was used to guide the conceptualization of improved data provision through a DPP and the standards used in data spaces. The framework by Jensen and colleagues [33] was applied to determine the gap between the existing data categories and types and the data required for a PCF. This helped to complement the framework by Jensen and colleagues with the necessary data to support sustainability management and enable Scope 3 reporting at the product level. In a final survey, the work process of the workshop and the results were reviewed by the researchers to reflect on the quality and plausibility of the outcomes. The researchers also conducted four subsequent interviews with the workshop participants to ensure the validity of the results regarding the concept.

4   Results

First, the current state of carbon accounting is outlined using corrugated board as an example. PackCorp is currently working on its annual sustainability report, and customers are increasingly demanding the PCF value. Because corrugated cardboard is mass-produced, the PCF refers to specific batches of cardboard. Sustainability managers are responsible for collecting the relevant Scope 1+2 data and performing PCF calculations in a web-based tool that complies with the applicable ISO standards (14067). The primary data from PackCorp's own operations must be entered into this tool. This tool has an interface to the SAP system, but a lot of other PCF-relevant input data (e.g. energy consumption, vehicle fleet, transport routes, etc.) must be entered manually.

Considering the input flows for each cardboard batch, the data on electricity, gas, purchased goods (i.e., base paper), additional materials (i.e., glue, ink), and internal transport must be determined. This data can be retrieved from an ERP system, and the production batch information can be retrieved from a MES. Some of the data on purchased goods can be retrieved using RFID scanners. However, the primary data on the transport routes for base paper and other data from the company's own mill boundaries are imprecise. Similarly, the data on external logistics is lacking and can only be estimated. PackCorp uses data from the industry association, which publishes a database with averaged data and a mixed value per ton of corrugated board for such blind spots in primary data. Therefore, the current process uses primary data from integrated source systems and averaged secondary data.

Accordingly, PackCorp's sustainability managers aim to move away from averaged values to improve the accuracy of the PCF and a DPP can support this. A DPP should have a standardized data model that supports the aforementioned data categories. All stakeholders in the corrugated board value creation system have access to contribute their data on the input flows that are relevant for carbon accounting. From PackCorp's perspective, this leads to eliminating the blind spots in the data on the base paper, as the paper mills submit their Scope 1+2 PCF for each base paper batch to the DPP. If the freight forwarders are integrated, the logistics-related emissions between paper mills, PackCorp, and retailers can be added to the PCF. With technologies such as the AAS and OPC UA (i.e., to gather machine data), and the EDC (i.e., to facilitate sovereign data sharing between enterprise software systems and the DPP), the necessary data can be collected effectively. Figure 2 illustrates how the enterprise software architecture changes between the current and enhanced state of carbon accounting supported by a DPP with environmental data.

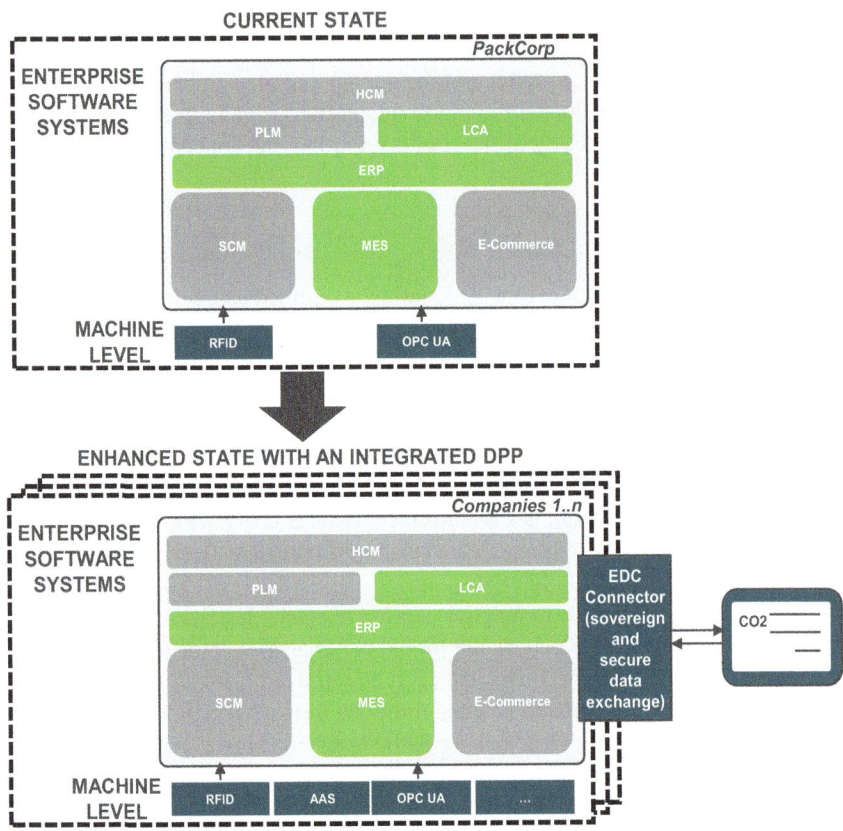

Fig. 2. Architectural comparison of the current state and the enhanced carbon accounting with a digital product passport fostering cross-organizational sharing of environmental data.

5   Conclusions, Limitations, and Future Research

5.1   Discussion of Key Findings

Recent research postulates that it is important to examine opportunities for data collection and analysis to foster sustainable decision-making [40]. Considering this, our study presents a scenario for a novel carbon accounting approach, which integrates a DPP for multiliterate data exchange between all value chain actors. The approach represents a significant step towards Scope 3 reporting. From a sustainability perspective, the approach shows that low-value tangibles, such as corrugated cardboard, can be considered in carbon accounting. In this scenario, the DPP acts as a central data hub for data-based collaboration to accurately calculate the PCF according to Scope 3. Figure 3 illustrates the role of a DPP in using environmental data from the raw material production, the cardboard production and the use of cardboard to realize scope 3 accounting.

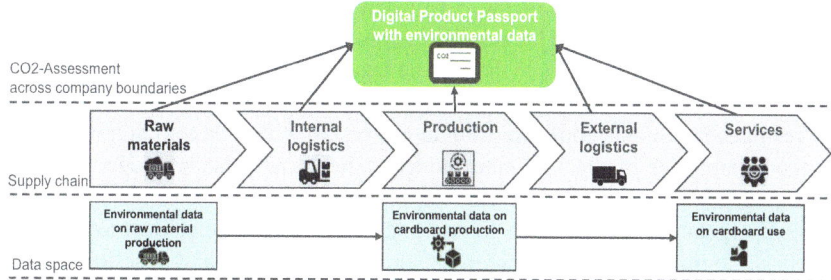

Fig. 3. Conceptual view on scope 3 accounting with a digital product passport.

PackCorp's experts confirmed that the end customer (e.g., a retailer) gains added value from a DPP, as it can store more data than only a calculated value and provide transparency about the calculation logic. Other supply chain companies can similarly find the PCF calculation logic. This helps to eliminate the divergences in accounting revealed by the DPP, so that the DPP helps enforce uniform accounting for a value creation system. In addition, PackCorp experts have confirmed that the DPP helps to fulfill new European legislation requirements such as *Packaging and Packaging Waste Regulations (PPWR)* or the aforementioned CSRD. Depending on the company's software landscape, the data model of a DPP can be extended. In the future, it is also possible to integrate waste (offcuts) into the PCF. However, Pack-Corp's experts have also pointed out that considering the current carbon accounting practices, the DPP would be based on historical data. Another uncertainty relates to the effort because the effort to gather data to calculate the exact values may be too high compared to the averaged values already available today. It is also unclear whether or not a DPP (i.e., its RFID tag or QR code) should be printed on each package.

From a technological perspective, the approach shows that the DPP can significantly reduce the efforts for sharing sustainability-related data by acting as a shared data model. Since a DPP also increases transparency, it can even help harmonize carbon accounting approaches, ultimately increasing company trust [36]. As a dataset, a DPP can be flexibly extended and tailored towards comprehensive reporting of carbon emission data of all actors throughout the entire value chain. A DPP can benefit from other digital solutions for data (e.g., digital twin) or connectivity (e.g., AAS or EDC). Although a DPP relies on establishing a data space, acting as a shared data model, it can also help overcome certain already challenges in data sharing that emerge in data spaces [14]. Overall, the scenario based on a beneficial interaction of a DPP and the enterprise software systems represents an improvement of the situation described for the use of environmental management information systems on the enterprise level [41].

5.2   Limitations

Our study is not without limitations. The first noteworthy limitation is related to the chosen research design, which is a single case study. Although we were able to capture the specific context of the corrugated cardboard industry, it is neither an industry where the DPP will be mandatory, nor is it an industry that produces high-tech products (such as batteries) that can be equipped with sensors to provide in-use data for the DPP. These aspects must be taken into account in the transferability of our results because this could have an impact on the willingness to invest and, thus, on the capabilities of the DPP and the associated enterprise software system for managing DPPs. These aspects also impact the potential data basis and also the sense of urgency in the industry. In addition, our data may be subject to interpretation bias. To mitigate this, the research team coded the internal discussions for each data issue and had the issues approved by data experts. However, the current state of implementation in the examined industry necessitated scenario thinking. Consequently, results such as concrete success factors for overcoming complex issues, such as negotiating which data should be collected across the supply chain and under what conditions when implementing DPPs [42], could not be clarified. For this reason, further research work needs to be carried out based on our study.

5.3   Future Work

In the long term, PackCorp aims to scale the presented digital sustainability context in the industry. In doing so, the concept will mature and create opportunities for design knowledge to abstract and de-abstract the concept so it can be applied to other products and industrial domains. The development of a carbon-accounting-oriented DPP will not only promote sustainability in the packaging industry but also lay a foundation for future data-driven business models. However, trust is an issue and is still not considered in the presented result. As there is no legal obligation to introduce the DPP in the corrugated cardboard domain, one prerequisite is to find a first-mover organization. With a first mover, a data space is implemented in a step-by-step process along the value chain (raw material supplier - cardboard manufacturer - cardboard customer). During the transformation of the value chain into a data space, a governance framework must be developed to ensure a fair use of data stored in a DPP. It will also be necessary to clarify whether, for example, the other actors will accept a first-mover company from the value chain as a data trustee in the emerging data space or whether an additional organization, acting as a data trustee to host DPPs, should be established. Therefore, future research must focus on a rule-based governance system [33, 43, 44] for the cross-company use of data and incentives for the supply chain actors to contribute their data to the DPP.

The use of other technologies that implement the governance system must also be researched further. The described scenario gave little consideration to the integration of connectivity technologies, such as the AAS or the EDC connection. These connectivity technologies can make a significant contribution to the efficient transfer of data from physical assets (e.g., machines) to DPPs. Similarly, the use of blockchain technologies also seems appropriate to ensure the integrity of the data stored in the DPP, due to the immutability of the data in the blockchain [45, 46]. however, the functioning of the blockchain may contradict the concept of data sovereignty, especially when data owners might wish to revoke the access or interrupt the data flow to the DPP. In blockchain, the data would be immutable once recorded, and only the review and approval by all the blockchain nodes would accomplish such a request. This means that control over the data is partially lost. Furthermore, the questions regarding the design of a backend system for managing the DPPs and the potential that machine learning can leverage from the sustainability data stored in a DPP are also still unexplored and represent a potential for future research.

References

1. Hart, S.L., A Natural-Resource-Based View of the Firm. The Academy of Management Review 20(4), 986-1014 (1995).
2. Hertwich, E.G., Wood, R.: The growing importance of scope 3 greenhouse gas emissions from industry. Environmental Research Letters 13, 104013 (2018).
3. Bielenia, M., Dubisz, D., Czermański, E.: Methodological introduction to the carbon footprint evaluation of intermodal transport. Frontiers in Environmental Science 11, 1237763 (2023).
4. Hettler, M., Graf-Vlachy, L.: Corporate scope 3 emission reporting as an enabler of supply chain decarbonization: A systematic review and comprehensive research agenda. Business Strategy and the Environment 33(2), 263-282 (2023).
5. Dahlmann, F., Rohrich, J.K.: Sustainable supply chain management and partner engagement to manage climate change information. Business Strategy and the Environment 28(8), 1632-1647 (2019).
6. Greenhouse Gas Protocol, https://ghgprotocol.org/sites/default/files/ghgp/standards/ghg-protocol-revised.pdf, last accessed 2024/10/28.
7. Jira, C.F., Toffel, M.W.: Engaging supply chains in climate change. Manufacturing & Service Operations Management 15(4), 559-577 (2013).
8. CDP, https://www.cdp.net/en/research/global-reports/global-supply-chain-report-2017, last accessed 2024/10/28.
9. Pirhonen, P., Nevala, A., Devireddy, S.: ABB: Driving a Sustainability Transformation with Process Intelligence. In: Reinkemeyer, L. (eds.) Process Intelligence in Action, pp. 75-85. Springer, Cham, München (2024).
10. Matthews, H.S., Hendrickson, C.T., Weber, C.L. The importance of carbon footprint estimation boundaries. Environmental Science & Technology 42(16), 5839-5842 (2008).
11. Krasikov P., Legner, C.: Introducing a Data Perspective to Sustainability: How Companies Develop Data Sourcing Practices for Sustainability Initiatives. Communications of the Association for Information Systems 53, 162-188 (2023).
12. Kotlarsky, J., Oshri, I., Sekulic, N.: Digital Sustainability in Information Systems Research: Conceptual Foundations and Future Directions. Journal of the Association for Information Systems 24(4), 936-952 (2023).
13. Neubauer, M., Steinle, L., Reiff, C., Ajdinović, S., Klingel, L., Lechler, A., Verl, A.: Architecture for Manufacturing-X: Bringing Asset Administration Shell, Eclipse Dataspace Connector and OPC UA together. Manufacturing Letters 37(12), 1-6 (2023).

14. Brechtel, M., Petrik, D., Hölzle, K.: From Challenges to Solution Pathways for Industrial Data Ecosystems. in: Proceedings of the Wirtschaftsinformatik, 48, AISeL, Paderborn (2023).
15. Cichy, P., Salge, T.O., Kohli, R.: Privacy concerns and data sharing in the internet of things: Mixed method evidence of connected cars. MIS Quarterly 45(4), 1863-1892 (2021).
16. Heil, M., Hoppe, H., Stein, T.: Softwareunterstützendes Nachhaltigkeits-Reporting. HMD 53, 721-735 (2016).
17. Fassnacht, M., Benz, C., Heinz, D., Leimstoll, J., Satzger, G.: Barriers to data sharing among private sector organizations. in: Proceedings of the 56th Hawaii International Conference on System Sciences, pp. 3695-3704, AISeL (2023).
18. Farahzadi, L., Mahdi, K.: Application of Machine Learning Initiatives and Intelligent Perspectives for CO2 Emissions Reduction in Construction. Journal of Cleaner Production 384, 135504 (2023).
19. Kabugo, J.C., Jämsä-Journela, S.L., Schiemann, R., Binder, C.: Industry 4.0 based process data analytics platform: A waste-to-energy plant case study. International Journal of electrical power & energy systems 115, 105508 (2020).
20. Catena-X, https://catena-x.net/de/about-us, last accessed 2024/11/10.
21. Catena-X, https://catena-x.net/de/angebote-standards/hmi-2023/circular-economy, last accessed 2024/11/10.
22. Jensen, S.F., Kristensen, J.H., Christensen, A., Waehrens, B.V.: An ecosystem orchestration framework for the design of digital product passports in a circular economy. Business Strategy and the Environment, 1-18 (2024).
23. European Commission, https://commission.europa.eu/energy-climate-change-environment/standards-tools-and-labels/products-labelling-rules-and-requirements/ecodesign-sustainable-products-regulation_en, last accessed 2024/11/10.
24. Paré, G., Trudel, M.C., Jaana, M., Kitsiou, S.: Synthesizing information systems knowledge: A typology of literature reviews. Information & management, 52(2), 183-199 (2015).
25. Bandara, W., Furtmueller, E., Gorbacheva, E., Miskon, S., Beekhuyzen, J.: Achieving rigor in literature reviews: Insights from qualitative data analysis and tool-support. Communications of the Association for Information systems, 37(1), 154-204 (2015).
26. Hahn, R.: Sustainability Management: Global Perspectives on Concepts, Instruments, and Stakeholders. 1st edn. (2022).
27. Jarke, M., Otto, B., Ram, S.: Data Sovereignty and Data Space Ecosystems. Business & Information Systems Engineering 61, 549-550 (2019).
28. Möller, F., Jussen, I., Springer, V., Gieß, A., Schweihoff, J.C., Gelhaar, J., Guggenberger, T., Otto, B.: Industrial data ecosystems and data spaces. Electron Markets 34, 41 (2024).
29. Hupperz, M., Gieß, A.: The Interplay of Data-Driven Organizations and Data Spaces: Unlocking Capabilities for Transforming Organizations in the Era of Data Spaces. in: Proceedings of the 57th Hawaii International Conference on System Sciences 2024 (HICSS-57), 2, Honolulu (2024).
30. Götz, T., Berg, H., Jansen, M., Adisorn, T., Cembrero, D., Markkanen, S., Chowdhury, T.: Digital Product Passport: The ticket to achieving a climate neutral and circular European economy?. University of Cambridge Institute for Sustainable Leadership (CISL) and the Wuppertal Institute, Cambridge (2022).

31. Langley, D.J., Rosca, E., Angelopoulos, M., Kamminga, O., Hooijer, C.: Orchestrating a smart circular economy: Guiding principles for digital product passports. Journal of Business Research 169, 114259 (2023).
32. Pohlmann, A., Popowicz, M., Schöggl, J.P., Bachler, J., Keler, J., Baumgartner, R.J.: Conceptualization of a digital product passport to enable circular and sustainable automotive value chains – the combustion engine use case. Procedia CIRP 122, 169-174 (2024).
33. Jensen, S.F, Kristensen, J.H., Adamsen, S., Christensen, A., Waehrens, B.V.: Digital product passports for a circular economy: Data needs for product life cycle decision-making. Sustainable Production and Consumption 37, 242-255 (2023).
34. van der Valk, H., Haße, H., Möller, F., Otto, B.: Archetypes of digital twins. Business & Information Systems Engineering 64, 375-391 (2022).
35. Schmidt, M., Moritz, N., Scholz, J.: Determining the Scope 3 Emissions of Companies. Chemical Engineering & Technology 45(7), 1218-1230 (2022).
36. Klaaßen, L., Stoll, C.: Harmonizing corporate carbon footprints. Nature Communications 12, 6149 (2021).
37. Dalkey, N. C., Brown, B. B., Cochran, S.: The Delphi method: An experimental study of group opinion. Santa Monica, CA: Rand Corporation (1969).
38. Liebig, B., Nentwig-Gesemann, I.: Gruppendiskussion. In: Kühl, S., Strodtholz, P., Taffertshofer, A. (eds.) Handbuch Methoden der Organisationsforschung, pp. 102-123. VS Verlag für Sozialwissenschaften (2009).
39. Tremblay, M. C., Hevner, A. R., Berndt, D. J.: Focus groups for artifact refinement and evaluation in design research. Communications of the association for information systems, 26(1), 599-618 (2010).
40. Schoormann, T., Strobel, G., Möller, F., Petrik, D., Zschech, P.: Artificial intelligence for sustainability—a systematic review of information systems literature. Communications of the Association for Information Systems, 52(1), 8, 199-237 (2023).
41. Leyh, C., Rossetto, M., Demez, M.:. Sustainability management and its software support in selected Italian enterprises. Computers in Industry, 65(3), 386-392 (2014).
42. European Parliamentary Research Service, https://www.europarl.europa.eu/RegData/etudes/STUD/2024/757808/EPRS_STU(2024)757808_EN.pdf, last accessed 2024/11/10.
43. Staub, N., Haki, K., Aier, S., Winter, R.: Governance Mechanisms in Digital Platform Ecosystems: Addressing the Generativity-Control Tension. Communications of the Association for Information Systems 52(1), 906-939 (2022).
44. Piétron, D., Staab, P., Hofmann, F.: Digital circular ecosystems: A data governance approach. GAIA-Ecological Perspectives for Science and Society, 32(1), 40-46 (2023).
45. Walden, J., Steinbrecher, A., Marinkovic, M.: Digital product passports as enabler of the circular economy. Chemie Ingenieur Technik, 93(11), 1717-1727 (2021).
46. Greiner, M., Seidenfad, K., Langewisch, C., Hofmann, A., Lechner, U. (2024). The Digital Product Passport: Enabling Interoperable Information Flows Through Blockchain Consortia for Sustainability. In: Phillipson, F., Eichler, G., Erfurth, C., Fahrnberger, G. (eds.) Innovations for Community Services. I4CS 2024. Communications in Computer and Information Science, vol 2109, pp. 377–396. Springer, Cham.

Generative Artificial Intelligence in Business Planning and Financial Budgeting

Dennis Schlegel[1][0000-0003-2484-5318] and Robin Fink[1]

[1] Reutlingen University, 72762 Reutlingen, Germany,
Dennis.Schlegel@Reutlingen-University.de

Abstract. Corporate planning and financial budgeting are essential for companies to achieve their long-term objectives. While the application of other technologies such as Robotic Process Automation (RPA) in planning and budgeting is already a well-established practice, the potential advantages of incorporating generative artificial intelligence (GenAI), specifically Large Language Models (LLMs) in the domain of planning and budgeting remain rather unclear. Hence, the aim of this research has been to identify potential use cases and review the current state of the discussion. A Multivocal Literature Review (MLR) was conducted to analyze and evaluate both academic and non-academic sources. The literature highlights the transformative potential of GenAI in enhancing business planning and financial budgeting through natural language interfaces, enabling users to access, analyze, and interpret data more effectively. However, the findings also show a gap in the existing academic literature and indicate that some grey literature sources may have to be interpreted with caution. Therefore, further research is required to fully understand and leverage the benefits of GenAI in corporate planning and budgeting.

Zusammenfassung. Unternehmensplanung und Budgetierung sind für Unternehmen wesentlich, um ihre langfristigen Ziele zu erreichen. Während die Anwendung anderer Technologien wie Robotic Process Automation (RPA) in der Planung und Budgetierung bereits gängige Praxis ist, sind die potenziellen Vorteile der Einbeziehung von generativer künstlicher Intelligenz (GenAI), insbesondere von Large Language Models (LLMs), in den Bereich der Planung und Budgetierung noch recht unklar. Ziel dieser Untersuchung war es daher, mögliche Anwendungsfälle zu identifizieren und den aktuellen Stand der Diskussion zu beleuchten. Es wurde ein Multivocal Literature Review (MLR) durchgeführt, um sowohl akademische als auch nicht-akademische Quellen zu analysieren und zu bewerten. Die Literatur unterstreicht das transformative Potenzial von GenAI bei der Verbesserung der Geschäfts- und Finanzplanung durch Schnittstellen in natürlicher Sprache, die es den Nutzern ermöglichen, effektiver auf Daten zuzugreifen, sie zu analysieren und zu interpretieren.

Die Ergebnisse verdeutlichen jedoch auch eine Lücke in der vorhandenen akademischen Literatur und zeigen, dass einige graue Literaturquellen kritisch zu hinterfragen sind. Daher ist weitere Forschung erforderlich, um die Vorteile von GenAI in der Unternehmensplanung und Budgetierung vollständig zu verstehen und zu heben.

Keywords: Budgeting, Business Planning, GenAI, LLM

1   Introduction

For companies, acting with foresight and adapting to different scenarios is essential in our dynamic environment of a globalized economy. Business planning is thereby a crucial component. The aim is to steer the entire company as well as sub-organizations in the desired direction and to ensure that the required resources are available [1]. According to [2], most of the authors referring to planning have in common that they describe planning as a purposeful, goal-oriented process that refers to future activities and involves an information processing process in which relevant knowledge is required.

While other AI-related technologies have gained increasing popularity in the fields of forecasting and budgeting [3], emerging AI technologies such as generative artificial intelligence (GenAI) have not yet been subject to the same level of attention. GenAI refers to deep-learning algorithms that are able to create new content based on the training data and an input prompt [4]. GenAI use cases are still to be determined, but GenAI could create additional value to existing AI technologies [5]. Therefore the aim of this paper is to investigate possible use cases of GenAI in business planning and budgeting applications and to critically review the state of research.

This paper is structured as follows. First, section 2 explains the background of planning and budgeting in business organizations. Next, section 3 discusses our research approach and the detailed design of the Multivocal Literature Review (MLR). Section 4 presents the results regarding potential use cases, before in section 5 key findings are formulated and the overall body of literature is critically discussed. Section 6 concludes the findings of this paper and gives further recommendations regarding future research.

2   Background

2.1   Business Planning and Financial Budgeting

Business planning aims to define execution actions in anticipation. This is also the difference to forecasting, as planning is strictly related to action. Planning is based on reflection (decision models) and intuition. Existing knowledge flows into the planning process and depending on the amount of that knowledge the relationship between reflection and intuition changes. Finally, planning also leads to the creation of plans and scenarios [2].

One of the challenges in planning is that companies have to build on the knowledge of many decision-makers. Overview knowledge must be combined with detailed knowledge. To simplify this, planning is typically carried out at three periodic levels. These include operational planning, tactical planning and strategic planning [2]. While strategic planning focuses on the long-term development of the company, operational planning is responsible for ensuring the short-term success [6]. Within an operational plan, a financial budget helps companies to coordinate their resources. [7] mention the following advantages of budget creation: A budget translates the corporate strategy into clear financial goals that all decision-makers in the company can follow. Managers must therefore consider the future and present a clear plan on how they want to achieve these goals. Different decision-makers in the company must coordinate with each other to coordinate sub-budgets. Finally budgeting creates comparability, as managers can compare the results actually achieved with the planned values [7].

2.2   Budgeting Process

There are several ways to proceed with operational planning. The top-down approach is based on the desired objectives of the management. However, problems can arise from employee dissatisfaction and foreseeable problems may only become apparent at a late stage. Bottom-up planning, on the other hand, involves setting objectives at lower levels and passing them upwards. Employees are often more satisfied, but the management's expected target level is often not achieved [6].

According to [7], the budgeting process starts with the corporate strategy, which is used to derive the sales forecast and the sales budget. Production quantities are then determined (taking into account stock levels and the sales budget). The production quantities serve as the basis for the production budget, which consists of the material cost budget, the manufacturing wage budget and the production overhead budget. In addition to the production budget, sub-budgets must also be formed for other departments such as administration or research. The profit budget ultimately results from these sub-budgets and results in a plan of the company's earnings. The cycle of this process is typically annual and involves the controlling department and those responsible for individual functions or product lines [7].

2.3   Data in Planning

When planning, it is particularly important to have reliable and accurate data. Companies often have a lot of data and it is not clear which of it is useful. As a planner, it is therefore important to filter out and use the relevant data from the mass of data. This requires specialist knowledge and expertise [8]. The two sources of information that are relevant for companies are information from internal and external areas. Internal sources of information include data from general accounting, cost accounting or internal statistics such as material statistics. External sources of information include publications from authorities, research reports, annual reports from other companies and market research results [8].

3   Research Method

We have conducted a MLR based on established guidelines [9, 10]. Since GenAI is a newer field of research [11], it is important to include grey literature (GL) in the literature review in addition to purely academic sources such as journal and conference papers. GL refers to literature that "[…] is produced on all levels of government, academics, business and industry in print and electronic formats, but which is not controlled by commercial publishers, i.e., where publishing is not the primary activity of the producing body." [9]. By including internal documents, preprints, and blog articles relating to GenAI, a broader and more up-to-date picture of the current state of research can be drawn [9]. This approach enabled the inclusion of information primarily from software providers (e.g. IBM and Jedox) and consulting firms (e.g. BCG) that have published whitepapers and articles regarding the topic of GenAI in planning and budgeting.

To ensure a systematic selection of the sources, the following inclusion and exclusion criteria have been developed [10].

- The literature must directly address the research aim.
- Only literature in English and German language is considered.
- Literature related to government financial planning is excluded.
- Literature related to personal financial planning is excluded.
- Literature that is too specialized in a specific industry is excluded.

In order to define the search string for our MLR, it is important to divide the research aim into individual areas. In this paper, research is undertaken in two separate areas, GenAI and business planning & budgeting, which are then combined to acquire new knowledge on how to leverage GenAI in the field of business planning and budgeting. After defining the individual areas, a list of synonyms, abbreviations, and alternative spellings is created to expand the search. Finally, the search string can be constructed using Boolean operators [10]:

- OR: to combine synonyms and alternative spellings
- AND: automatically applied within Google Scholar through parentheses

Using this process, the following search string was obtained and applied to Google Scholar:

*allintitle:("GenAI" OR "Artificial Intelligence" OR "AI" OR "GPT" OR
"ChatGPT" OR "LLM" OR "Large Language Model") ("Integrated Business Plan-
ning" OR "Operational Controlling" OR "Business Planning" OR "Budgeting" OR
"Financial Planning" OR "Operational Planning" OR "Corporate Planning" OR
"Budget Forecasting")*

In addition to the literature found on Google Scholar, a general Google search
was conducted. According to [9], the usage of a general web search engines like
Google is valid and practiced in the context of software engineering and management research. The Google search complements the Google Scholar search, which
primarily includes academic literature, with GL [9]. The quality of search results
can decline quickly using the Google search engine, that is why possible stopping
criteria include theoretical saturation, the inclusion of only top N search results and
evidence exhaustion [9]. For the GL search in the Google search engine, a limit of
50 search hits has been set for this research, which is a suitable size [12, 13].

The search string then has been applied to Google Scholar where 52 results were
displayed (excluded citations). Four results that are not available in English nor German have been excluded in the beginning. This left 45 results, from which 20 the
title was not suitable to the RQ. Further 19 results have been excluded due to an
unsuitable abstract. Ultimately, only five full-text sources based on the Google
Scholar search were included in the MLR [14–18]. Based on the general web search
with Google, seven additional sources [19–25] were included, so that a total of 12
sources were included in the MLR.

4   Results on Use Cases

4.1   Natural Language Interface

[19] envisions that GenAI "[...] has the potential to empower users to access
descriptive, diagnostic, predictive and prescriptive insights through natural language in a conversational experience." [19]. Also [24] emphasizes the opportunity
of using GenAI to communicate with the planning tool in natural language. This
approach enables "information consumers and business analysts [to] access meaningful auto-generated visualizations and self-serve rich insights using natural language" [24]. SAP's GenAI Co-Pilot Joule can answer "[...] questions or frame a
problem in plain language." [24].

BCG also identifies the advantage in NLP, as "AI may also help executives en-
vision novel human-machine interfaces for planning, such as conversation-based
ones." [22]. A conversational interface could lead to more users being able to "[...]
have access to information, insights and personalized recommendations [...]" [19].
The natural language interface enables users to make "[...] financial data more accessible and understandable through natural language queries and voice recognition" [20].

4.2   Supporting Decision Making

When making strategic decisions, like optimized budget allocation, further insights regarding the objectives can improve the outcome of these decisions [19]. GenAI can help decision makers and companies to "[...] help make informed decisions and deliver better business outcomes." [19]. This could be implemented in such a way that the user asks questions about certain expenditures, and the GenAI additionally lists the most important influencing factors. By explaining the provided data, the user can better understand which steps in the planning process can have what effects on other processes. It also saves decision-makers time, as they receive high-quality information without having to spend a lot of time analyzing data [19].

Also [15] mentions how optimized resource allocation can be supported "[...] by analyzing historical expenditure patterns, identifying cost-saving opportunities, and predicting future spending needs."

4.3   Improved Planning Models

[24] mentions one use case of GenAI in scenario planning. On their website they state that "planners can model a wide range of future scenarios and generate more accurate forecasts and plans" [24]. [15] as well mark the possibility to quickly adapt to different market dynamics: "AI's adaptability to market dynamics and aptitude for capturing intricate relationships are clear advantages." [15]. In the white paper by IBM, they also state that they want to leverage AI "[…] to enable users to identify risks and opportunities and accelerate business agility proactively." [19]. According to [14], AI could help to further identify cause-and-effect relationships within value chains. This could possibly help managers to create optimized spending patterns. AI assists "[...] to realize the ideal number of sales professionals or to identify diminishing marginal utility and to predict purchasing decisions of customers including their influencing factors." [17].

[25] claim that "GenAI predicative planning leverages AI to analyze past data and recognize trends, patterns, and correlations, resulting in more accurate forecasting" [25].

4.4   Integrating Unstructured Data

Both [15] and [17] mention the advantages of analyzing unstructured data sources utilizing AI. Thereby information from "[...] news or blog articles and posts in social media" [15] can be used to gain insights which then could have an influence in the budgeting decision.

"Through NLP techniques, AI can generate coherent and contextually relevant explanations for deviations from forecasts and budgets." [15], this leads to saved time and also enables the finance professionals to rather work on the important topics, which require more thought [15].

[17] mention a use-case, where algorithms are used to gain information about the capital structure of their competitors, and used those to evaluate target settings for the future. Management then can use this information for their own planning process. Also the mining of text to gain information of reports, which then are summarized and presented to the management, helps in faster decision making [17]. NLP can be used to "[...] better identify the expectations and needs of stakeholders to support evidence-based decision making." [17].

[22] emphasize, that customized GenAI systems "[...] could near-instantly scan through thousands of data points and provide insights, in natural language, about past changes in sales trends, the outliers in historic data, the reasons for sales acceleration or deceleration, and new growth opportunities." [22]. As well data quality can be enhanced and AI based planning models can be tuned and updated [22]. [23] states that these types "[...] of unstructured data or derived judgement has always been theoretically available to make use of in the forecasting process [...]" [23] but was just not used in an efficient way. He is of the opinion that due to "[...] the advancement in computer vision, natural language processing, and semantic modelling through LLM, now offers the promise [...][to] extract and structure at scale content of this design [...]" [23].

4.5 Automation of Data Collection and Purification

Some papers do not refer directly to GenAI, but still provide useful recommendations for the usage of AI in planning and budgeting. These include automation, data collection and, data purification. [16] states that AI reduces time-consuming, as well as labor-intensive tasks, involving data collection, aggregation, and purification. By taking on these tedious and time-consuming, but not really demanding tasks, planners have more time to concentrate on their key tasks. AI opens the possibility to "[...] streamline planning and financial reporting, as well as evaluate thousands of data points in real time [...]" [16]. The time saving aspect of automated data processing helps "employees [to] save time avoiding repetitive tasks and use their knowledge and skills in more value-added activities, like data analysis." [18]. [21] came to the same conclusion: "AI can automate time-consuming tasks, freeing up teams to concentrate on the more valuable aspects of their roles." [21].

[15] also mention the importance of automating the collection, preprocessing and allocation of data through the utilization of AI. Through the automation, the risk of manual errors can be reduced as well as the efficiency increased [15].

[14] refer to a study, that underscores AIs ability to "[...] automate routine tasks, thereby enhancing the accuracy and efficiency of financial reporting." [14].

5   Discussion and Key Findings

Based on our review of the publications, the following key findings can be summarized regarding the state of research in the field:

First, in the academic sphere, there is a lack of literature that specifically refers to GenAI in business planning and financial budgeting. While this is not surprising given the novelty of the topic, it should be noted that even in the larger field of AI as a superset of GenAI, there are only few sources on the topic of AI in planning and budgeting. This has also been previously noted by [3], who states that there are "surprisingly few publications of machine learning applications" [3] in the field of Financial Planning and Analysis (FP&A). Also [17] describe the state of AI in the finance profession as being in its infancy, pointing out the necessity for more real-life examples to fully understand the opportunities and challenges presented by AI.

Second, the GL provides more potential use cases than the academic literature. In the Google search results, most entries were from consultancies supporting the digital transformation of their client firms [22, 25], as well as from technology providers promoting their GenAI solutions [21, 24]. With hindsight, this also supports the choice of our research method of the MLR. However, we should be critically aware that GL has only moderate credibility and outlet control [9], given the commercial interest of the players involved.

Third, the interpretation of the results should take into account the fact that AI is in its early stages [17] and is constantly evolving [15] and therefore, the results are only a snapshot in time. Further research is becoming increasingly important. Still, general directions can be derived from the literature, which are also applicable to the use of GenAI, particularly LLMs.

Fourth, readers of this paper should note that many of the use cases discussed in the (grey) literature are hypothetical and the practicability may have to be proven in the future. This is also related to the fact that sometimes there seems to be a confusion of terminology or misconception about GenAI's actual capabilities. For example, the use case of more accurate forecasting is actually more characteristic of predictive analytics within machine learning rather than GenAI. Another problem is that many of the statements made in publications are very generic and have to be further operationalized into more specific use cases, e.g. the commonly formulated notion that AI frees employees from tedious tasks and enables them to concentrate on value-adding activities. Given the fact that many AI projects in organizations fail due to unrealistic expectations based on misunderstandings of AI capabilities by decision makers [26], buzzwording or bullshitting (as defined by [27]) about use cases and benefits of GenAI may nurture such misunderstandings and should rather be avoided.

6   Conclusion

In conclusion, this paper contributes to the understanding of the emerging role of GenAI in business planning and financial budgeting. By systematically identifying and critically discussing both academic and non-academic sources, we have synthesized previously dispersed knowledge.

Our research has important implications for both, practitioners and academics. Practically, the review has shown that GenAI may provide interesting use cases and benefits for planning and budgeting applications. At the same time, this research calls for caution against overhyping AI capabilities, advocating for a critical reflection and thorough understanding of GenAI's possibilities and limitations in planning processes. Scientifically, it underscores the need for further empirical research to bridge the gap between hypothetical use cases and real-world applications. Due to the limited number of academic publications and the growing interest in the topic by software providers [21, 24], consulting firms [22], and other industry sectors, it is important to continue research on use cases of GenAI in planning and budgeting. This also includes the choice of further research methods, such as expert interviews, which reveal increased insights into companies and the usage of GenAI in planning and budgeting.

References

1. Handel, H.: Unternehmensplanung mit SAP Analytics Cloud. Rheinwerk Verlag; Rheinwerk, Bonn (2021)
2. Weber, J., Schäffer, U.: Einführung in das Controlling. Schäffer-Poeschel Verlag, Stuttgart, Freiburg (2022)
3. Wasserbacher, H., Spindler, M.: Machine Learning for Financial Forecasting, Planning and Analysis: Recent Developments and Pitfalls (2021)
4. Martineau, K.: What is generative AI?, https://research.ibm.com/blog/what-is-generative-AI
5. McKinsey & Company: Economic potential of generative AI | McKinsey, https://www.mckinsey.com/capabilities/mckinsey-digital/our-insights/the-economic-potential-of-generative-ai-the-next-productivity-frontier#key-insights , Accessed 31 July 2024
6. Britzelmaier, B.: Controlling. Grundlagen, Praxis, Handlungsfelder. Pearson, München (2020)
7. Friedl, G., Hofmann, C., Pedell, B.: Kostenrechnung. Eine entscheidungsorientierte Einführung. Franz Vahlen, München (2022)
8. Ehrmann, H., Mintert, S.: Unternehmensplanung. Kiehl, Herne (2022)
9. Garousi, V., Felderer, M., Mäntylä, M.V.: Guidelines for including grey literature and conducting multivocal literature reviews in software engineering (2017)
10. Kitchenham, B., Charters, S.: Guidelines for performing Systematic Literature Reviews in Software Engineering (2007)
11. McKinsey & Company: What is generative AI?, https://www.mckinsey.com/featured-insights/mckinsey-explainers/what-is-generative-ai , Accessed 31 July 2024
12. Kulesovs, I.: iOS Applications Testing. ETR 3, 138–150 (2015)

13. Tom, E., Aurum, A., Vidgen, R.: An exploration of technical debt. Journal of Systems and Software 86, 1498–1516 (2013)
14. Addy, W.A., Ajayi-Nifise, A.O., Bello, B.G., Tula, S.T., Odeyemi, O., Falaiye, T.: Transforming financial planning with AI-driven analysis: A review and application insights. World J. Adv. Eng. Technol. Sci. 11, 240–257 (2024)
15. Jain, V., Kulkarni, P.A.: Integrating AI Techniques for Enhanced Financial Forecasting and Budgeting Strategies. SSRG-IJEMS 10, 9–15 (2023)
16. Kunnathuvalappil Hariharan, N.: Artificial Intelligence and human collaboration in financial planning (2018)
17. Marotta, G., Au, C.-D.: Budgeting in the Age of Artificial Intelligence – New Opportunities and Challenges. SSRN Journal (2022)
18. Massaro, M., Bagnoli, C., Albarelli, A., Dal Mas, F.: Business Planning and Artificial Intelligence: Opportunities and Challenges for Accounting Firms in a Human-Centered Perspective, 327–337 (2024)
19. Andrade, R. de: The future of business planning with generative AI - IBM Blog, https://www.ibm.com/blog/the-future-of-business-planning-with-generative-ai/ , Accessed 31 July 2024
20. Bapat, D.: AI & Financial Planning – How the Former Enhances the Latter, https://escalon.services/blog/ai-financial-planning-how-the-former-enhances-the-latter/, Accessed 31 July 2024
21. Jedox: How to explore integrated business planning with ChatGPT, https://www.jedox.com/en/blog/ibp-chatgpt/ , Accessed 31 July 2024
22. Klein, L., Saxena, A., Mallet, T., Shetty, A., Bouffault, O., Sack, D. and Wegman, R.: AI Can Transform Integrated Business Planning, https://www.bcg.com/publications/2023/ai-driven-integrated-business-planning-platforms
23. Portnoy, R.: AI Use Cases – Why AI and Business Planning should be Happy Bedfellows, https://www.linkedin.com/pulse/ai-use-cases-why-business-planning-should-happy-roger-portnoy-kwzue, Accessed 31 July 2024
24. SAP: Generative AI for analytics and planning, https://www.sap.com/germany/products/technology-platform/cloud-analytics/features/generative-ai.html, Accessed 31 July 2024
25. Shuttleworth, H., Khan, S. and Russell, K.: How CFOs can transform their Financial Planning and Analysis through Generative AI, https://www.wolterskluwer.com/en-gb/expert-insights/wb-generative-ai-financial-planning-transformation-cfo#form#gc , Accessed 31 July 2024
26. Westenberger, J., Schuler, K., Schlegel, D.: Failure of AI projects: understanding the critical factors. Procedia Computer Science 196, 69–76 (2022)
27. Frankfurt, H.G.: On bullshit. Princeton University Press (2005)

Exploring the Role of Techno-Overload, Techno-Complexity and Involvement Facilitation on End-User Experience in Utilizing Digital HR Tools

Soufinaz Baharestani[1] and Hasan Koç[1][0000-0002-1614-0230]

[1] Berlin International University of Applied Sciences, Salzufer 6, 12524 Berlin, Germany
soufinazbaharestani,koc@berlin-international.de

Abstract. Digital transformation affected Human Resources (HR) processes, and have brought a high variety of digital HR tools to the market in order to facilitate and increase the process efficiency. This study examines the experiences of non-HR employees in organizations that utilize digital HR tools, which provide various functions, including submitting absence requests, accessing payroll documents, and managing employee performance. In particular, we examine the potential impact of the digital HR tools on non-HR end-user experience, focusing on the technostressors, techno-overload and techno-complexity, as well as the moderating role of involvement facilitation on the user satisfaction, measured through the End-User Computing Satisfaction (EUCS) model. Data from 99 participants show that techno-complexity negatively influences four of five key aspects of user satisfaction, including content, format, ease of use, and accuracy, while techno-overload has no significant impact. Involvement facilitation moderates the adverse effects of techno-complexity, improving user perceptions of format and accuracy.

Zusammenfassung. Die digitale Transformation hat die Prozesse im Personalwesen (HR) beeinflusst und eine Vielzahl digitaler HR-Tools auf den Markt gebracht, um die Prozesseffizienz zu erleichtern und zu erhöhen. Diese Studie analysiert die Erfahrungen von Mitarbeitern außerhalb des Personalwesens mit digitalen HR Tools. Diese Tools bieten Funktionen zur Abwesenheitsplanung, Gehaltsabrechnung und Leistungsverwaltung. Insbesondere untersuchen wir die potenziellen Auswirkungen der digitalen HR-Tools auf die Endnutzererfahrung von Mitarbeitern, die nicht im Personalwesen tätig sind, wobei wir uns auf Technostressoren,Techno-Overload und Techno-Komplexität sowie auf die moderierende Rolle der Beteiligungsförderung (Involvement Facilitation) auf die Nutzerzufrieden-heit konzentrieren, die anhand des End-User Computing Satisfaction (EUCS)-Modells gemessen wird. Daten von 99 Teilnehmern zeigen, dass Techno-Komplexität vier von fünf Schlüsselbereichen der Nutzerzufriedenheit negativ beeinflusst, darunter Inhalt, Format, Benutzerfreundlichkeit und Genauigkeit, während Techno-Overload keine signifikanten Auswirkungen hat.

© Der/die Autor(en), exklusiv lizenziert an
Springer Fachmedien Wiesbaden GmbH, ein Teil von Springer Nature 2025
M. Möhring et al. (Hrsg.), *Herman Hollerith Conference 2024*, Informatik aktuell,
https://doi.org/10.1007/978-3-658-48215-2_7

Die Beteiligungsförderung moderiert die negativen Auswirkungen der Techno-Komplexität und verbessert die Nutzerwahrnehmung von Format und Genauigkeit.

Keywords: Technostress, Involvement Facilitation, Digital HR Tools, End-User Experience.

1   Introduction

Digital transformation plays a central role in today's businesses, fundamentally re-shaping the way organizations operate. Digital transformation is defined as "the integration of digital technology into all aspects and operations of an organization, which in turn leads to infrastructural changes in how the organization is operated and delivers value to its customers" [1, p.2]. Although digital transformation extends beyond merely implementing new technologies, tools, digital systems and software implementation plays a central role in transforming today's organizations.

In organizational management, the transformation of Human Resources (HR) practices by digital means has become an important trend. To facilitate the management of the HR functions, organizations adapt digital systems, termed as Human Resources Information Systems (HRIS) [2]. These digital HR tools streamlined HR processes, such as Artificial Intelligence (AI)-based employee onboarding [3], talent management [4], data-driven planning [5], and performance management [6], offering an improved user experience for employees and managers [7][8].

However, it is undeniable that these digital tools also bring up certain challenges, such as the pressures of adapting to new systems, micromanagement and technostress, which in turn affect employee satisfaction and productivity [9][10]. Studies show that employees may experience increased stress levels due to the demands of learning new systems, managing information overload and adapting to continuous technological changes [11][12]. In the context of the digital HR tool use, such challenges can be intensified for non-HR employees, who generally have fewer affordances than HR employees and often perceive HR tools as intrusive [10]. Additionally, non-HR employees may lack the familiarity and comfort with digital HR tools that HR professionals, who rely on them extensively, tend to have. However, there is a lack of studies on how techno-stressors affect end-user experience among this group.

For a successful implementation and use of the digital HR tools, empirical evidence underlines the importance of workforce's ability to adapt, supported by adequate ICT resources [13]. Providing robust ICT support and aligning tools' capabilities with organizational goals and employee needs are other important factors [13][7]. Against this background, the main objective of this study is to assess which aspects of digital HR tools affect end-user experience in non-HR employees, and to propose strategies to improve the success of implementing digital HR tools. In particular, the research questions are: i) From the digital HR tools perspective, what is the role of the technostressors in the context of end user experience for non-HR employees? ii) How does the perception of the technostressors change in this group with the mediating role of involvement facilitation for the digital HR tools? By evaluating the experiences of non-HR employees as end users, this study aims to provide insights into improving the implementation of digital HR tools. Highlighting the importance of managing technostress and increasing involvement facilitation [8][9], the findings will help organizations enhance the effectiveness of their HR processes through digital tools [13][10], and extend the body of knowledge on technostress and HR tools from a non-HR-staff perspective [14].

2   Literature Review

2.1   Digital Transformation in Human Resources Management

Traditional HR functions have been changed fundamentally due to the digital transformation of HR, by integrating advanced technologies. Implementing digital HR tools have enhanced operational efficiency, decision-making, and strategic alignment, reshaping the HR processes. HRIS simplify workflows and reduce manual tasks with developing automation in functions such as payroll, performance management, and recruitment [15][16][7]. These tools also improve workforce planning, employee engagement, and talent management, by offering real-time data analytics [17]. Integrating different aspects of digital tools, including cloud-based HR platforms, AI-driven tools, and HR analytics, provides HR professionals with the opportunity to make more sophisticated decisions, and contribute to organizational goals [18][19].

Research on the impact of digital HR tools shows that these technologies improve the end-user experience by enhancing efficiency, communication, and accessibility [20][16]. Improved user interaction with HR processes within these digital tools, offers self-service options which lead to empowering employees in managing their tasks more efficiently and flexibly [21][22]. The usability and performance of HRIS, along with comprehensive training, are directly correlated with user satisfaction, affecting system usage and efficiency, specifically in time-sensitive tasks like absence management [16].

Besides, customized learning paths, training programs, and benefit management in digital HR tools enhance personalized employee experiences [17][23], support continuous development and increase engagement [24]. However, digital HR adoption also presents challenges, including technostress, skills gaps, and a slow uptake of digital tools in some sectors [9][19], mainly in cases where the technology is implemented deficiently or lacks sufficient user support [14]. For instance, segmented digital implementations focusing on separate HR processes—such as recruitment or time planning—creates redundancies across systems and hindering a holistic approach to digitalization, leading to limited overall process efficiency [25].

Although non-HR employees are also the users of digital HR tools, the current literature has overlooked their user experience. These users may have distinct characteristics that set them apart from HR professionals or other organizational stakeholders as some studies also indicate different attitudes between these two groups of HR and non-HR employees [26]. For instance, they may have varying levels of technological proficiency, different job demands, technological affordances and frequency interaction. We argue that a separate perspective on Digital HR tools can help researchers understand these user characteristics and their implications for tool design and implementation, addressing an important gap in the literature on digital HR transformation [24].

2.2   Technology Acceptance and Technostress

Studies indicate that although face-to-face interactions continue to play a crucial role in building relationships within HR [27], digital HR tools enhance both organizational outcomes and employee satisfaction by boosting communication, flexibility, and access to resources [28]. Yet, adoption of new technologies, especially in a high pace, introduces challenges. One such challenge is technostress, referring to the stress experienced by employees when adapting to digital systems [9]. Technostress has five dimensions, of which techno-overload and techno-complexity are among the most studied in the literature [29]. Techno-complexity addresses the effort of learning and understanding tools to reduce complexity. Techno-overload is the "pressure to work faster or more due to technology" [29, p. 8]. Technostress is associated with both psychological and behavioural outcomes. This investigation focuses on the non-HR staff end user experience with the HR tools as a behavioural outcome.

In defining technostress management strategies, one important moderator is the organisational usage context of technology [29]. Studies show that technical support provision, involvement facilitation, and literacy facilitation help mitigate technostress [9][29]. ICTs' usability and reliability can reduce perceived work overload, while dynamic and intrusive features of these technologies often increase it, highlighting the importance of stable, user-friendly HR tools to mitigate stress [31]. Promoting digital literacy, being aligned with traditional HR practices, and planning for employees to be well equipped for managing these technologies, are further strategies mentioned in the literature [32][33]. Organizations can improve performance expectancy by giving employees a clear image of how new HR tools can improve their job performance. This can be reached by offering adequate training and resources, making the transition to digital tools smoother [34]. Negative consequences of technostress can be alleviated if the training is promoted continuously, including robust ICT support systems and ongoing skill development [31][32].

Organizations may employ technology acceptance models that provide insights into how digital HR tools can be more effectively adopted. End User Computing Satisfaction (EUCS) is one such model. It concentrates on measuring user satisfaction with specific aspects of a system, i.e. content (relevance and appropriateness of the information provided by the HR tool), format (presentation of information within the HR tool), ease of use (intuitiveness of the HR tool), accuracy (correctness of the information provided by the HR tool) and timeliness (promptness with which information is delivered to users) [35].

3   Research Methodology

The study examines the impact of technostress and involvement facilitation in shaping non-HR employees' experiences, as end-users, with digital HR tools. The study narrows down on two dimensions of technostress—techno-overload and techno-complexity. Involvement facilitation is a crucial variable in mitigating technostress and enhancing user experience [30]. The research model integrates the EUCS for measuring end-user experience with five dimensions [35], and is depicted in Fig. 1.

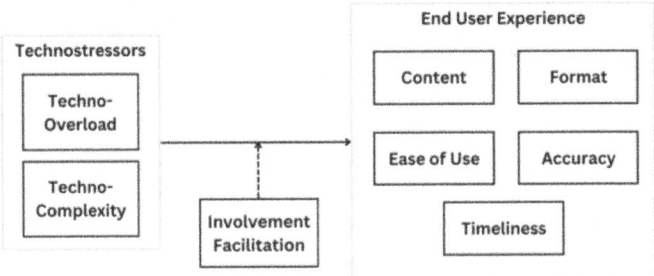

Fig. 1. Research Model

The study adopts a quantitative approach, implementing a survey to measure the dimensions shown in   Fig. 1. The survey collected data on the gender (Male: 50.51%, Female: 49.49%), education levels (High school: 4.04%, Two-year college: 4.04%, Bachelor's degree: 33.33%, Master's degree: 48.48%, PhD degree: 10.10%), and tool experiences of the participants (M=4.73 years, SD = 4.18). To increase the quality of responses, we also incorporated an attention check question. Furthermore, two open-ended questions about the experiences with the HR tool were asked to gather input for the strategies to improve the HR tool user experience. The data collection process was conducted online and anonymous, and the questionnaire took approximately 4-6 minutes to complete. The survey targeted non-HR/non-admin employees in organizations who use digital HR tools. It was distributed in our network and via Prolific, and 99 valid responses were analyzed. As for the constructs used in the study, "techno-overload" (alpha: 0.83) and "techno-complexity" (alpha: 0.87) was measured with five questions each following [30]. The involvement facilitation was measured with four items (alpha: 0.82). For measuring the end user experience, we utilized the EUCS scale [35]. A total of eight questions measured accuracy (alpha: 0.80), timeliness (alpha: 0.84), ease of use (0.76) and format (0.81). Finally, content was measured with four items (alpha:0.92). All items were measured using a five-point Likert scale.

4   Results

After controlling for the effects of gender, education and tool experience, techno-overload did not significantly predict any of the first-level dimensions of the EUCS model. On the contrary, techno-complexity significantly and negatively predicted content (b = −0.280, t(91) = −3.471, p<.001), format (b = −0.118 , t(91) = −2.506, p = .014), ease of use (b = −0.101, t(42) = −2.366, p=.02) and accuracy (b = −0.10, t(91)=−3.254, p=.002). Only the timeliness construct was not significantly predicted at the standard alpha level of 0.05. For brevity reasons, Table shows only the significant paths and the control variables.

Table 1. Results of the regression analysis (with significant paths only)

| | Dependent variable: | | | |
	Content	Format	Ease of Use	Accuracy
TCO	**-0.280*****	**-0.118***	**-0.101***	**-0.100****
Gender	1.029	0.448	0.326	0.264
Education-TwoYear	-1.784	-1.250	-1.334	**-2.979****
Tool Experience	0.099	0.068	0.047	**0.157*****
Education-Bachelor	-0.784	0.198	0.412	-0.599
Education-Master	-2.841	-0.758	-0.430	-1.218
Education-PHD	-2.058	-0.167	-0.413	-1.365
Constant	18.911***	8.763 ***	8.657***	9.181***
Observations	99			
R^2	0.301	0.256	0.214	0.150

Translating these findings into the practice, users experiencing high techno-complexity, e.g. due to a lack of computer skills or requiring to spend more time to learn an HR tool, feel that the information provided by the HR tool has a lower quality and is less relevant to the their needs. Due to the negative association with the format variable, these users are likely to perceive that the outcomes of the HR tool are not presented in a useful format and are less clear. Similarly, users experiencing higher techno-complexity might rather think that the HR tool employed is not easy to navigate and operate, potentially leading to lower task accomplishment rate. Last but not least, they rely on the data accuracy less, feeling less confident when making an informed decision.

We also ran a moderation analysis to investigate whether involvement facilitation interacts with techno-complexity when put in context with the four different outcomes. Moderation was shown up by a significant interaction effect between techno-complexity and format (b = 0.024, 95%CI [0.008, 0.040], t = 2.934, p = .004), as well as techno-complexity and accuracy (b = 0.021, 95%CI [0.001, 0.042], t = 2.100, p = .039). No significant interaction effects are found between techno-complexity, ease of use and content. The simple slopes visualizing the results of the analysis are shown in Fig. 2.

Table 2. Involvement Facilitation as a "protective role"

Outcome variable	Slope at -1SD of Moderator	Slope at +1SD of Moderator
Accuracy	-0.157	-0.114
Format	-0.195	-0.147

Increased techno-complexity is associated with decreased accuracy and format satisfaction, regardless of the level of involvement facilitation. For both outcomes, the negative relationship between techno-complexity and the outcome (accuracy or format) is weaker when involvement facilitation is high (+1 SD) compared to when it is low (-1 SD). Supporting the technostress literature, this indicates that involvement facilitation indeed acts as a buffer, reducing the negative impact of techno-complexity on both accuracy and format satisfaction. From a practical perspective, the moderating effect of involvement facilitation suggests that it plays a protective role in the relationship between techno-complexity and user satisfaction in terms of accuracy and format (see Table 2).

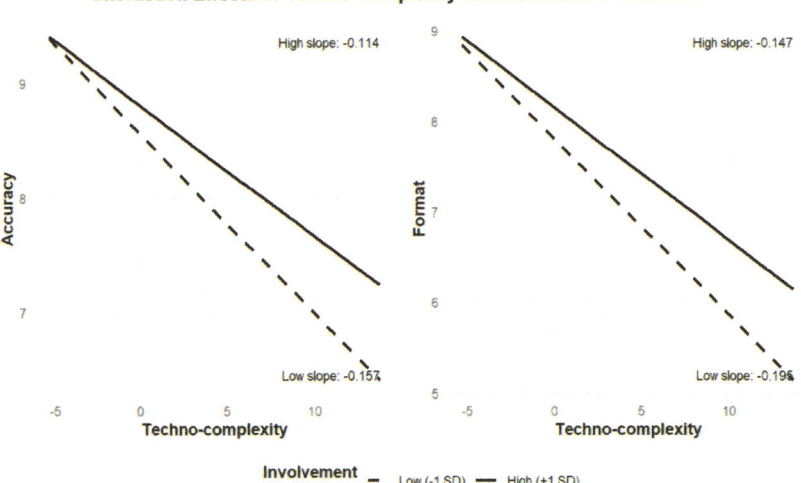

Fig. 2. The moderating impact of involvement facilitation

5   Discussion and Implications

The results of this study emphasize the notable impact of technostress, particularly techno-complexity, on satisfaction for digital HR tools end-users, as measured by the EUCS model. The analysis shows that techno-complexity significantly and negatively affects four out of five dimensions of EUCS, including content, format, ease of use, and accuracy. On the contrary, techno-overload did not show a significant impact on user satisfaction, suggesting that the amount of tasks or information is not as disadvantageous to user experience as the perceived complexity of the tools.

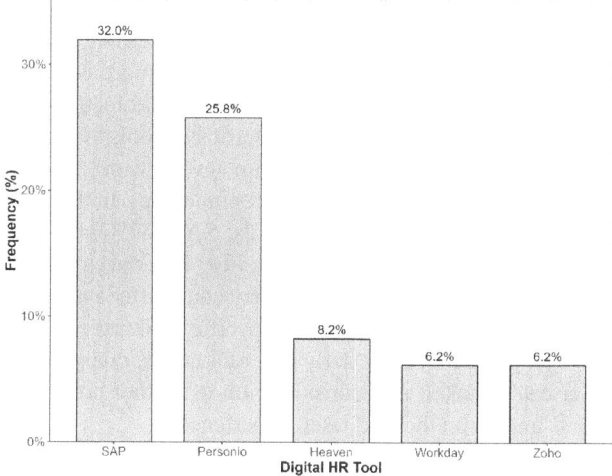

Fig. 3. Top-5 tools used in our sample

Examining the moderating role of involvement facilitation, the results indicate that it can act as an alleviator, specifically in mitigating the negative effects of techno-complexity on format and accuracy satisfaction. The findings show that users with higher involvement facilitation were less affected by the negative consequences of tools' complexity, specifying improved satisfaction with the format and accuracy of the HR tool. Responses to the open-ended questions in the survey also support this finding. Participants mentioned having more training, interactive user guides, or tutorials to help them better manage the technology use. From a practical perspective, this highlights the importance of ensuring an ongoing support to help non- HR employees navigate the techno-complexity, leading to higher levels of user satisfaction. Also, several respondents addressed the necessity of involving the employees by asking them "what they really need", offering "a better introduction" or showing the benefits of the tool. Thus, the organizations are recommended to understand the requirements of the non-HR users before implementing an HR tool, and align it with the business needs.

Another key implication of the study is that digital HR tool companies should consider designing more user-friendly, adaptable interfaces, allowing personalized content and reporting options for end-users of these tools as their customers. Providing non-HR employees with the ability to customize dashboards and reports based on their specific needs can help them access relevant information efficiently, reducing the time spent navigating systems. Additionally, simplifying workflows, enabling automated notifications, and offering real-time alerts for unverified entries may enhance usability, reduce errors and alleviate technostress for non-HR employees.

6   Limitations

Future studies could develop findings in this study by dealing with some limitations of the current research. First, the sample size of 99 participants, while being adequate for an analysis, limits the generalizability. Expanding the survey sampling across different industries or sectors could provide a more comprehensive understanding of the issue. Additionally, future research could focus on studying the impact of technostress within the context of specific HR tools to compare user experiences, or investigate one digital HR tool from several aspects, such as comparing end-user experience between HR and non-HR employees. In this study, participants were users of more than five digital HR tools, SAP (32%) and Personio (25.8%) being the most frequently adapted tools (see Fig. 4). Concentrating on one or two widely used digital tools in a particular industry could offer a more detailed analysis and allow for more practical and industry-specific recommendations. Finally, further variables such as the weekly/ daily HR tool usage, computer self efficacy, or digital mindset can be taken into consideration as further potential moderators of technostressors' impact on the End User Experience.

References

1. Kraus, S., Durst, S., Ferreira, J. J., Veiga, P., Kailer, N., & Weinmann, A.: Digital transformation in business and management research: An overview of the current status quo. International Journal of Information Management, 63, Article 102466 (2022). https://doi.org/10.1016/j.ijinfomgt.2021.102466
2. Vrontis, D., Christofi, M., Pereira, V., Tarba, S., Makrides, A., & Trichina, E.: Artificial intelligence, robotics, advanced technologies and human resource management: A systematic review. The International Journal of Human Resource Management, 33(6), 1237–1266 (2022). https://doi.org/10.1080/09585192.2020.1871398
3. Jedel, I., & Palmquist, A.: Factors related to the use and perception of a gamified application for employee onboarding. In: Ahram, T., Taiar, R., & Groff, F. (eds.) Human Interaction, Emerging Technologies and Future Applications IV. IHIET-AI 2021. Advances in Intelligent Systems and Computing, vol 1378, pp. 877-885. Springer, Cham (2021). https://doi.org/10.1007/978-3-030-74009-2_83
4. Cuesta-Valiño, P., Kazakov, S., Henche, B.G., & Núñez-Barriopedro, E.: The application of artificial intelligence in recruitment, training, and employee onboarding HR practices. In: Del Val Núñez, M.T., Yela Aránega, A., & Ribeiro-Soriano, D. (eds.) Artificial Intelligence and Business Transformation. Contributions to Management Science, pp. 193-208. Springer, Cham (2024). https://doi.org/10.1007/978-3-031-58704-7_13
5. Margherita, A.: Human resources analytics: A systematisation of research topics and directions for future research. Human Resource Management Review, 32(2), Article 100795 (2022). https://doi.org/10.1016/j.hrmr.2020.100795
6. Sardi, A., Sorano, E., Garengo, P., & Ferraris, A.: The role of HRM in the innovation of performance measurement and management systems: A multiple case study in SMEs. Employee Relations, 43(2), 589-606 (2021). https://doi.org/10.1108/ER-03-2020-0101

7. Murugesan, U., Subramanian, P., Srivastava, S., & Dwivedi, A.: A study of artificial intelligence impacts on human resource digitalization in Industry 4.0. Decision Analytics Journal, 7, Article 100249 (2023). https://www.elsevier.com/locate/dajour

8. Sudirjo, F., Ekasari, S., Hendayani, N., Dharmawan, D., & Launtu, A.: Application of the end user computing satisfaction method to analyze user satisfaction toward the quality of mobile banking services. Jurnal Informasi dan Teknologi, 6(1), 150-154 (2024). https://jidt.org/jidtt

9. Tarafdar, M., Tu, Q., & Ragu-Nathan, T. S.: Impact of technostress on end-user satisfaction and performance. Journal of Management Information Systems, 27(3), 303-334 (2010). https://doi.org/10.2753/MIS0742-1222270311

10. Fedorova, A., Koropets, O., & Gatti, M.: Digitalization of HRM practices and their impact on employee's well-being. In: Digitalization of Business Processes: Trends, Challenges, Solutions, pp. 145-157. Springer (2019). https://doi.org/10.1080/09585192.2017.1363796

11. Baluch, A. M.: Employee perceptions of HRM and well-being in nonprofit organizations: unpacking the unintended. The International Journal of Human Resource Management 28(14), 1912–1937 (2016). https://doi.org/10.1080/09585192.2015.1136672

12. Nielsen, K., Nielsen, M. B., Ogbonnaya, C., Känsälä, M., Saari, E., Isaksson, K.: Workplace resources to improve both employee well-being and performance: A systematic review and meta-analysis. Work & Stress 31(2), 101–120 (2017). https://doi.org/10.1080/02678373.2017.1304463

13. Gavrilidou, G.: Impact of super user support on user perceptions and satisfaction with integrative technologies: A social presence perspective (Ph.D. thesis). McMaster University, DeGroote School of Business (2023).

14. Florkowski, G. W.: HR technologies and HR-staff technostress: an unavoidable or combatable effect? Employee Relations 41(5), 1120-1144 (2019). https://doi.org/10.1108/ER-08-2018-0214

15. Melnychenko, S., Lositska, T., Bieliaieva, N.: Digitalization of the HR-management system of the enterprise in the context of globalization changes. Financial and Credit Activities: Problems of Theory and Practice 6(41), 534-543 (2021).

16. Hamid, J. A., Johannes, Y., Yacob, S., Edward.: The effectiveness of human resource information system through employee satisfaction and the system usage. Put It Right Journal (PIRJ) 1(1), 29-46. Doctoral Program in Economics, Faculty of Economics and Business, Universitas Jambi (2022).

17. Murphy, A.: Can the digitisation of HR services alter employee perceptions of those services and the HR function at the same time as delivering HR operational cost savings to an organisation? Master's dissertation, Dublin Business School (2018).

18. Cen, F., Ali, D. A.: Improving the organizational efficiency of manufacturing enterprises: The role of digital transformation, resource planning (ERP), and business practices. Journal of Law and Sustainable Development 12(13) (2024). https://doi.org/10.55908/sdgs.v12I3.2439

19. Njoku, E., Ruël, H., Rowlands, H., Evans, L., Murdoch, M.: An analysis of the contribution of e-HRM to sustaining business performance. In: HRM 4.0 for human-centered organizations, vol. 23, pp. 21-39. Emerald Publishing Limited (2020). https://doi.org/10.1108/S1877-636120190000023003

20. Nandy, A., Basu, R.: Role of HR digitisation in personalization of employee benefit. Srusti Management Review 12(2), 28-35 (2018).

21. Barisic, A. F., Rybacka Barisic, J., Miloloza, I.: Digital Transformation: Challenges for Human Resources Management. ENTRENOVA - Enterprise Research Innovation 7(1), 357-366 (2021). doi:10.54820/GTFN9743

22. Kirilmaz, S. K.: Digital transformation in human resources management: investigation of digital HRM practices of businesses. Research Journal of Business and Management (RJBM) 7(3), 188-200 (2020). https://doi.org/10.17261/Pressacademia.2020.1282

23. El-Guindy, Y., Safwat, T., Kadry, M.: Impact of digital transformation adoption on non-financial performance metrics in Egyptian technology firms. International Journal of Business and Technology Studies and Research 6(1) (2024). http://www.ijbtsr.org

24. Zhang, J., Chen, Z.: Exploring human resource management digital transformation in the digital age. Journal of the Knowledge Economy 15(4), 1482–1498 (2024). https://doi.org/10.1007/s13132-023-01214-y

25. Mitrofanova, E. A., Konovalova, V. G., & Mitrofanova, A. E.: Opportunities, problems, and limitations of digital transformation of HR management. The European Proceedings of Social & Behavioural Sciences EpSBS, GCPMED 2018 International Scientific Conference "Global Challenges and Prospects of the Modern Economic Development", 1717–1727. Future Academy. https://dx.doi.org/10.15405/epsbs.2019.03.174

26. Tyagi, V. K.: Balancing Notice Periods: An Empirical Study of HR and Non-HR Perspectives (2023). http://dx.doi.org/10.2139/ssrn.4647565

27. DiRomualdo, A., El-Khoury, D., & Girimonte, F.: HR in the digital age: How digital technology will change HR's organization structure, processes and roles. Strategic HR Review, 17(5), 234–242 (2018). https://doi.org/10.1108/SHR-08-2018-0074

28. Suwaji, R., Muliyadi, M., Kusuma, A.: The Role of HR Technology in HR Management Transformation: Improving Organisational Efficiency and Productivity. Jurnal Informasi dan Teknologi 6(2), 83-91 (2024). https://jidt.org/jidt

29. Nastjuk, I., Trang, S., Grummeck-Braamt, J.-V., Adam, M. T. P., & Tarafdar, M. (2023). Integrating and Synthesising Technostress Research: A Meta-Analysis on Technostress Creators, Outcomes, and IS Usage Contexts. European Journal of Information Systems, 1–22.

30. Tarafdar, M., Tu, Q., Ragu-Nathan, B. S., Ragu-Nathan, T. S.: The impact of technostress on role stress and productivity. Journal of Management Information Systems 24(1), 301-328 (2007). https://doi.org/10.2753/MIS0742-1222240109

31. Ayyagari, R., Grover, V., Purvis, R.: Technostress: Technological antecedents and implications. MIS Quarterly 35(4), 831-858 (2011). https://doi.org/10.2307/41409963

32. Bengtsson, C., Bloom, M.: Human resource management in a digital era: A qualitative study of HR managers' perceptions of digitalization and its implications for HRM. Master's thesis, Lund University, School of Economics and Management (2017).

33. Fernandez, V., Gallardo-Gallardo, E.: Tackling the HR digitalization challenge: Key factors and barriers to HR analytics adoption. Competitiveness Review: An International Business Journal (2019). https://doi.org/10.1108/CR-12-2019-0163

34. Sarfaraz, J.: Unified theory of acceptance and use of technology (UTAUT) model-mobile banking. Journal of Internet Banking and Commerce 22(3) (2017). http://www.icommercecentral.com

35. Doll, W. J., Torkzadeh, G.: The measurement of end-user computing satisfaction. MIS Quarterly 12(2), 259-274 (1988).

Potentials and Risks of the Low-Code Development: A Systematic Literature Review

Stefan Trieflinger[1], Dimitri Petrik[2][0000-0002-0244-1235], Ebru Polat[3],
and Bastian Roling[4]

[1] University of Reutlingen, Altenburgstr. 150, 72762 Reutlingen, Germany
stefan.trieflinger@reutlingen-university.de
[2] Graduate School of Excellence Advanced Manufacturing Engineering (GSaME), University of Stuttgart, Nobelstr. 12, 70569 Stuttgart, Germany
dimitri.petrik@gsame.uni-stuttgart.de
[3] University of Stuttgart, Keplerstr. 17, 70174, Stuttgart, Germany
ebru.polat@bwi.uni-stuttgart.de
[4] viastore Systems GmbH, Magirusstr. 13, 70469, Stuttgart, Germany
b.roling@viastore.de

Abstract. Low-code development and deployment have become increasingly popular in recent years and is now used by many organizations. By providing a simple and user-friendly interface for creating source code, these low-code can significantly reduce the time and cost of developing digital applications. With low-code, software applications can be implemented quickly without requiring in-depth programming skills. This democratization of software development presents significant opportunities but also introduces risks, creating a trade-off for IT governance. This paper aims to examine this trade-off by conducting a systematic literature review of the growing body of literature, specifically focusing on the challenges and potentials of low-code adoption. The results include an overview of the reported challenges and potentials. They can be used in practice by organizations weighing the pros and cons of low-code implementation and governance. Furthermore, the results provide a basis for formulating a research agenda at the organizational level.

Zusammenfassung. Low-Code-Entwicklung und -Bereitstellung sind in den letzten Jahren immer beliebter geworden und werden inzwischen von zahlreichen Unternehmen eingesetzt. Durch die Bereitstellung einer einfachen und benutzerfreundlichen Schnittstelle für die Erstellung von Quellcode kann Low-Code die Zeit und die Kosten für die Entwicklung digitaler Anwendungen erheblich reduzieren. Mit Low-Code kann Anwendungssoftware schnell implementiert werden, ohne dass tiefgreifende Programmierkenntnisse erforderlich sind. Diese Demokratisierung der Software-Entwicklung bietet erhebliche Chancen, birgt aber auch Risiken, die für die IT-Governance einen Trade-Off darstellen.

© Der/die Autor(en), exklusiv lizenziert an
Springer Fachmedien Wiesbaden GmbH, ein Teil von Springer Nature 2025
M. Möhring et al. (Hrsg.), *Herman Hollerith Conference 2024*, Informatik aktuell,
https://doi.org/10.1007/978-3-658-48215-2_8

In diesem Beitrag wird dieser Trade-Off anhand einer systematischen Analyse der wachsenden Zahl von Literatur untersucht, wobei der Schwerpunkt
auf den Herausforderungen und Potenzialen der Low-Code-Einführung liegt.
Die Ergebnisse umfassen einen Überblick über die beschriebenen Herausforderungen und Potenziale. Sie können in der Praxis von Organisationen ge-
nutzt werden, die die Vor- und Nachteile einer Low-Code-Implementierung
und Governance abwägen. Darüber hinaus bieten die Ergebnisse eine Aus-
gangsbasis für eine Forschungsagenda auf betrieblicher Ebene.

Keywords: Low-code, low-code platforms, challenges, potentials, systematic literature review.

1   Introduction

Over the years, companies have had only two options when it comes to app development: Buying existing apps from an external provider or developing them entirely
in-house and having them customized by experienced developers and programmers
[1]. Nowadays, low-code, and recently no-code development approaches are on the
rise and provide users across the organization with access to application development capabilities. With the ever-increasing innovation speed, companies are challenged to create and operate increasing numbers of digital services, processes, and
products to sustain a competitive advantage [2]. Digitalization not only offers the
potential to develop products and services to meet customer needs, but also the opportunity to improve internal operations. Examples include implementing digital
workflows and providing applications or services to internal stakeholders [3, 4].
However, many companies face the challenge of finding people with the right skills
and expertise to complete these projects [4].

One way to address this challenge is to use the low-code development approach,
where software development is based on a virtual user interface without requiring
advanced skills in the relevant programming languages. According to a study by
Gartner [5], the global market for low-code development will grow by 22.6% between 2020 and 2021, indicating that, in practice, 70% of digital development is
now done using low-code technology [6]. Embracing low-code development, companies expect certain benefits, such as cost optimization or more efficient progress
in developing digital products [7]. However, low-code development is not always
unproblematic, and numerous organizational issues can arise [8]. The diverse challenges and potentials make the decision to use low-code complex for an organization's IT. The use of low-code in companies is still a relatively new phenomenon,
so it can be assumed that not all potentials and challenges are yet known [9]. Because of this and the wide range of potential applications for using low-code development, the scientific community is increasingly interested in this topic and the
number of publications on low-code is increasing [10].

Considering this, this paper aims to structure this growing body of knowledge
and provide an overview of the potentials and challenges of low-code from the organizational perspective, which is already recognized in scientific research.

Therefore, this paper reports an extensive literature analysis that focuses on discussing organizational potentials and risks of introducing low-code.

2   Related Work

The term low-code was first introduced by market analysis company Forrester in 2014, conceptualizing low-code development as a platform-based software development approach that enables the creation of applications with minimal hand-coding by relying on visual development environments and declarative programming interfaces [11] with code being automatically created in the background, resulting in applications or services [8]. Low-code is based on fundamental principles and ideas from model-driven software development. This involves the use of automation, analysis, and modeling options, which in turn are made possible by the use of modeling and meta-modeling [12].

Well-known software vendors like IBM, Microsoft, or Oracle offer low-code platforms [9], so other organizations can adopt these platforms. Within a detailed literature review, Pinho et al. [13] found that ten features characterize low-code programming. The primary characteristic is that software development is carried out by employees from different departments ("non-programmers") and by non-competent experts. These users are also called citizen developers with little IT knowledge and are employed in specialist departments within an organization. Empirical results indicate that low-code helps organizations leverage bottom-up digital innovation, improve processes, and create more applications for external and internal use [7]. In line with this, low-code platforms can be used in various domains, including the energy industry, healthcare, banking and insurance, telecommunications, and manufacturing. Low-code applications are also used for business processes related to human resources, logistics, sales, project management, and manufacturing [14].

An obvious advantage of low-code is the acceleration and rationalization of software development. This can promote digitalization in organizations [15]. Departments can use low-code to design self-service applications and digitize processes. This can reduce dependence on IT. Following this, departments are no longer tied to software developers, alleviating the shortage of IT experts from central IT departments. Given this, low-code development is even seen as an approach that democratizes software development [16]. This variety of possibilities in using low-code, which can extend to critical business processes in the most diverse organizational contexts, requires adequate governance in the organizational context, as otherwise they can lead to problems [17]. Against this background, a number of studies have already been produced that analyze the potentials and risks of low-code, which are not immediately obvious [e.g., 7, 18]. To structure this growing field, this article aims to analyze the existing literature to derive challenges and potentials relevant to organizations.

3   Research Approach

The aim of this paper is to give an overview and synthesize the potentials and challenges of low-code development at the organizational level. In order to achieve this aim, we defined the following research questions:

- **RQ1:** What potentials of using low-code in organizations are reported in the scientific literature?

- **RQ2:** What risks of using low-code in organizations are reported in the scientific literature?

To perform a systematic literature review, we combined the approach from Brocke et al. [19] for a systematic search on the database level with Webster and Watson's approach [20] to organize the literature sample in a conceptual matrix.

Data sources: The procedure of conducting a systematic literature review is intended to be well-defined to ensure that it is objective and repeatable. To answer the research questions, scientific publications were searched in the cross-publisher databases Ebscohost and Scopus. In addition, the publisher databases IEEE Xplore, SpringerLink, and AiSeL were added. A final search was carried out through Google Scholar.

Search strings and study selection: As a first step in our search, we identified a list of search terms during a brainstorming session and by screening conceptual papers to understand the topic. In order to cover our research questions and obtain sufficient results, we iteratively developed the search terms. After discussing various options, we defined the following search term:

(„(Low-Code OR LCDP) AND (development OR platform OR citizen developer)") We screened all the papers (i.e., reading the titles and abstracts of the papers) returned by the databases Ebscohost, Scopus, IEEE Xplore, and AiSeL. However, due to high hit numbers, we relied on the ranking algorithm for SpringerLink, Scopus, and Google Scholar and screened only the first 200 hits, because after that, the relevance of the hits decreased significantly. Hence, according to Cooper's taxonomy, the literature analysis cannot be considered exhaustive but representative [21].

After screening and assessing the full texts, our search yielded a sample of 31 papers. After performing subsequent forward and backward searches, we added 11 more papers to the sample. As a result, the final sample comprises 42 papers. To build the literature sample, we relied on the pre-codification scheme, proposed by Bandara and colleagues [22]. The study selection process is illustrated in Figure 1:

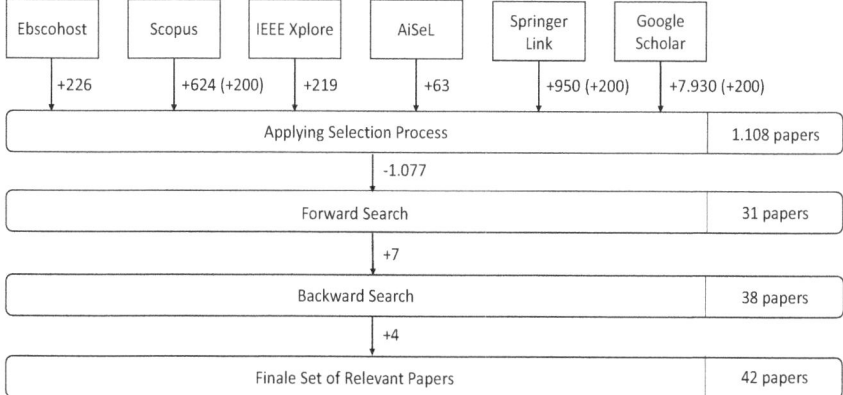

Figure 1. Study selection process.

During the screening process, we applied the following inclusion and exclusion criteria:

Inclusion:

- Papers published in the scientific databases Ebscohost, Scopus, IEEE Xplore, SpringerLink, and AiSeL. This includes journal and conference publications.
- The language of the publication is written in English.
- The full text of the publication is available.

Exclusion

- Papers that do not focus on the topic of low-code challenges or potentials but rather mention low-code occasionally.
- Publications that were not peer-reviewed and grey literature.
- Publications presenting the same results of another study in various papers (i.e., indicated by cross-citations), or written by the same authors. In such a case, only one publication was included in the sample.

4   Results

To answer the research questions, we analyzed the relevant articles describing the potentials and risks of low-code development. The identified potentials and risks are presented in the following subsections. The inductively created concept matrix can be viewed here: https://bit.ly/3XHKDAv

4.1   Potentials (RQ1)

Cloud-based development: Low-code platforms are hosted in the cloud, including a drag-and-drop functionality for the implementation, a preview of software applications, and a cloud-based deployment of applications. Therefore, software developers do not need to install any tools or libraries for the applications to run. As a result, the use of low-code fosters the usage of cloud services within organizations. Consequently, low-code development advances the digitalization of organizations [23].

Shorter development times: Rafiq, Filippo, and Wang et al. [23] pointed out that the introduction of Low-Code can lead to shorten development time in contrast to conventional software development. As the main reasons, the authors identify the implementation of rapid feedback cycles and the reduction of the workload for developers [7]. Sahay et al. [12] point out that a high level of abstraction, combined with operation in a cloud-based platform, also shorten the development time because the low-code platform deals with the issues of maintainability, scalability, and extensibility.

Job satisfaction: Li et al. [24] conducted empirical research showing that job satisfaction increases when employees collaborate using low-code. By restructuring tasks in terms of individual needs and affiliations, employees' satisfaction increases. When an activity is completed with LCDP, there is a role change in the software project. Employees are not only seen as customers of an application but also as collaborators. In turn, satisfaction employees increases as the employees are proactively involved in the implementation of applications and have contributed to the implementation [7]. The IT department can also be relieved of the burden of developing simple applications, which leads to greater satisfaction in the IT department [25].

Foster the Alignment between Business and IT: Low-code enables employees with a technical background and employees without a technical background to transfer and execute the corporate strategy in the IT infrastructure. For this, low-code provides a common language that forms the basis for discussions between various departments and across all hierarchical levels. Therefore, the introduction of low-code fosters the alignment between business and IT and can contribute to breaking down silos [26].

Promoting digital change and transformation: Furthermore, low-code lowers the barrier for employees to familiarize themselves with and use low-code. In addition, multiple solutions can be quickly developed, deployed, tested, and then either abandoned for something else or adopted [10]. Low-code is, therefore, described in several articles as promoting digital change through a trial-and-error approach.

Cost reduction: By using low-code, development cycles can be shortened. This not only enables a faster market launch but can also create competitive advantages and generate additional profit [27]. This reduces both integration costs and expenditure on future IT projects. Furthermore, the visual development environment also simplifies the creation of applications, meaning that a software application may be achieved with fewer staff, making software development more cost-efficient. Internal developers can relieve themselves of recurring tasks with low-code, which also positively changes the cost structure within an organization [28].

4.2   Risks (RQ2)

Interoperability risks: Prinz et al. [29] reported that scaling is an emerging risk. In particular, the author points out that low-code development platforms have a lack of open standards. Therefore, two distinctive organizations can implement different interfaces and deploy incompatible data models, as low-code platforms do not standardize these applications. Therefore, a lack of interoperability is expected between applications created with low-code [7].

Technical debt and security risks: Moreover, the author points out that regular data retrieval by the low-code platforms from the organization involved in low-code development requires their protection from unauthorized access, eventually leading to compliance and security gaps. In this context, a major risk is if a department implements the introduction of low-code platform without the knowledge from IT [29]. Yan [30] confirms that once dependencies to low-code platforms exist, the data is vulnerable to data breaches. In particular, a common reason is that the platform providers do not fully monitor data protection measures and the associated codes. For example, a major risk is if the platform provider does not carry out any or only a few security updates. In such a case, companies are forced to invest in individual platforms, which leads to an increase in cost [30]. Furthermore, low-code development code testing can be restricted, which may comprise the security of an application and lead to technical debt in the future [7].

Lack of acceptance: Another hurdle is that developers do not always accept the use of low-code [29]. One reason for this is that the use of low-code can prevent the use of the full technical potential [7]. In particular, low-code development is not the most suitable approach for developing innovative solutions. One possible way of using low-code is the business process automation. An IT department could, for instance, use forms, workflows, and authorization logic to automatically assign licences to employees. This is because the drag-and-drop functionalities of low-code platforms offer fewer possibilities than conventional programming development. Therefore Naqvi et al. [31] point out that developers can be observed rejecting the use low-code in their projects, as they are passionate about participating in creative software development projects without the restrictions set by the low-code development platform [31].

Vendor lock-in: Elshan et al [7] state that starting the implementation of low-code on a platform results in dependency on the low-code vendor. On the one hand, there is the risk that each platform provider relies on its own application implementation ecosystem. For example, a Mendix application cannot be developed or integrated into the Microsoft Power Platform. Therefore, once the decision for a platform provider has been made, transferring the low-code project to another platform is impossible. If a change of the platform provider is technically possible. Sufi [26] points out that none of the existing low-code platforms enable integration with minimal effort. Therefore, if the platform is changed, the entire low-Code project must be redesigned and implemented on the new platform from scratch. Therefore, migrating between platforms is technically impossible and economically not viable [26].

Initial invest, training, and resources: Furthermore, introducing low-code cannot be purposeful without sufficient knowledge management. However, companies face the challenge of finding employees with sufficient knowledge about low-code development and skills in specific low-code platforms to offer ongoing trainings for the employees. Consequently, introducing low-code demand for finding and involving the "right" people necessitates an ongoing effort associated with staff training and further education [31].

Determination of the total costs: A further risk is determining the total costs, especially over a long period of software development and operations based on low-code. This risk is exacerbated by the fact that low-code vendors offer different billing models and can increase prices anytime. Therefore, Prinz et al. [29] recommend keeping dependencies on low-code platform providers as low as possible.

Lack of flexibility: Finally, when implementing low-code is a lack of flexibility. As low-code platforms usually do not provide advanced features for complex software projects (e.g., code repository management or other tools for team collaboration) or requirements, its use is limited to small software projects. Moreover, the low-code modules are usually defined and preconfigured, which lowers the flexibility of using low-code compared to those developed conventionally [4, 30].

Table 1. Overview of potentials and risks of the use of low-code

Potentials	Risks
• Cloud-based development	• Interoperability risks
• Shorter development times	• Compliance and security risks
• Foster the Alignment	• Lack of acceptance
• Promoting digital transformation	• Vendor lock-in
• Cost reduction	• Initial invest, training, and resources
• Job satisfaction	• Determination of the total costs
	• Lack of flexibility

5   Conclusion and Future Research

The performed systematic literature analysis yielded in 42 hits. Although the number of risks in Table 1 exceeds the number of potentials, we conclude that low-code development is a purposeful approach but must be managed carefully. Although citizen development can ignite bottom-up innovation and advance digitalization within an organization, it requires certain control and governance mechanisms. As mentioned above, low-code platforms can still demand IT knowledge from citizen developers, especially if the intended software bears a certain complexity. Hence, a launch of low-code development in organizations without sufficient assistance from IT departments can quickly lead to unpredictable outcomes related to the aforementioned risks. It is important for companies to introduce a standardized process for the release of low-code applications, in particular, to prevent shadow IT and not to lose track of bottom-up innovations.

Consequently, our analysis shows that introducing low-code in organizations is subject to innovation-control tension. One exemplary measure to establish control is the provision of sufficient training materials and educational programs [15]. On the other hand, existing research indicates that developers tend to reject low-code [7], although developers (i.e., from IT departments) need to be involved to take over projects from citizen developers before the final release to perform quality assurance or to develop certain functionalities. Given the lack of acceptance, we conclude that additional tensions between business and IT departments must be mitigated not to jeopardize business IT alignment at the human level.

In addition, governance of low-code is necessary, as low-code development is intended for rather simple problems and software projects and can help with the digitalization of processes. However, it also forces innovation into the limits of the functionalities supported by low-code platforms. However, the IT department can also use low-code for its own benefit and design certain labor-intensive processes with low-code in order to reduce its own workload.

To conclude, low-code necessitates new governance tasks, and a literature-based comparison of potentials and risks helps identify these. However, the study is also subject to certain limitations. The first limitation of our study is the applied stopping condition. After 200 hits in each library, we stopped the screening process, relying on the database algorithms. Accordingly, in line with [21], we cannot claim that the analyzed sample is exhaustive, but rather representative. In any case, we could not find any empirical studies in our sample that were dedicated to formulating success factors. Success factors should have a guiding effect and be formulated according to the cause-effect scheme. At the same time, success factors should explain mechanisms for achieving the goal in sufficient detail, and situational factors influencing success should be uncovered as much as possible [32, 33]. The lack of success factors could provide decision-makers in practice with guidance on the management of innovation-control tensions and, therefore, represents a gap that future studies should address.

The second noteworthy limitation of our study stems from the applied research design, which includes only scientific literature. This means that only highly aggregated results were analyzed, and the latest insights from the practice are not included. In order to increase the validity of our results, we discussed our findings with one practitioner who has several years of experience in the use and introduction of low-code. However, a follow-up study should include grey literature and analyze experience reports from the practice to examine the possible expectation-confirmation gaps after introducing low-code in organizations more closely. The research team plans interviews and surveys with representatives from IT departments regarding their governance mechanisms and processes and how low-code affects their work routines. Another opportunity for future research is to conduct domain-specific studies and determine how low-code performs in industries affected by certain constraints, such as manufacturing, highly regulated industries, or governmental institutions.

References

1. SAP, What is low-code/no-code application development?, https://www.sap.com/products/technology-platform/build/what-is-low-code-no-code.html, last accessed 2024/09/.
2. Elshan, E., Dickhaut, E., Philipp, E.: An Investigation of Why Low Code Platforms Provide Answers and New Challenges. In: Proceedings of the Hawaii International Conference on System Sciences (ICSS) (2016).
3. Krejci, D., Iho, S., Missonier, S.: Innovating with employees: an exploratory study of idea development on low-code development platforms. In Proceedings of the European Conference on Information Systems (ECIS), pp. 1-16, AISeL (2021).
4. Käss, S.: Low Code Development Platform Adoption: A Research Model. In ACIS 2022 Research Papers, pp. 1-5, AISeL (2022).
5. Magic quadrant for low code applications, https://appian.com/learn/resources/resource-center/analyst-reports/2023/gartner-magic-quadrant-for-low-code-2023, last accessed 2024/09/.
6. Liu, D., Jiang, H., Guo, S., Chen, Y., Qiao, L.: What's Wrong With Low-Code Development Platforms? An Empirical Study of Low-Code Development Platform Bugs. In IEEE Transactions on Reliability, pp. 695-709, IEEE (2023).
7. Elshan, E., Germann, D., Dickhaut, E., Li, M.: Faster, Cheaper, Better? Analyzing How Low Code Development Platforms Drive Bottom-Up Innovation. In Proceeding of the European Conference on Information Systems (ECIS), pp. 1-17 (2023).
8. Luo, Y., Liang, P., Wang, C., Shahin, M., Zhan, J.: Characteristics and Challenges of Low-Code Development: The Practitioners' Perspective. In: Proceedings of the 15th ACM/IEEE International Symposium on Empirical Software Engineering and Measurement (ESEM), pp. 1-11 (2021).
9. Bock, A. C., Frank, U.: Low-Code Platform. Business & Information Systems Engineering 63, 733 – 740 (2021).
10. Bucaioni, A., Cicchetti, A., Ciccozzi, F.: Modelling in low-code development: a multivocal systematic review. Software and Systems Modeling 21.5, 1959 – 1981 (2022).
11. Richardson, C., Rymer, J. R., Mines, C., Cullen, A., Whittaker, D.: New development platforms emerge for customer-facing applications. Forrester: Cambridge, MA, USA, 15. (2014)
12. Sahay, A., Indamutsa, A., Di Ruscio, D., Pierantonio, A.: Supporting the understanding and comparison of low-code development platforms. In: 46th Euromicro Conference on Software Engineering and Advanced Applications (SEAA), pp. 171-178, IEEE (2020).
13. Pinho, D., Ademar, A., Vasco, A.: What about the usability in low-code platforms? A systematic literature review. Journal of Computer Languages 74 101185 (2023).
14. Hinrichsen, S., Adrian, B.: Potenziale der Low-Code-Programmierung für Industriebetriebe. In: Prozesse in Industriebetrieben mittels Low-Code-Software digitalisieren: Ein Praxisleitfaden, pp. 1-16, Springer Berlin Heidelberg (2023).
15. Carroll, N.: The Importance of Citizen Development for Digital Transformation. Cutter IT Journal 34.3, 5 – 9 (2021).
16. Prinz, N., Huber, M., Riedinger, C., Rentrop, C.: Citizen Development als Treiber der digitalen Transformation – Aktuelle Ansätze bei der Adoption von Low-Code Development Plattformen. In: HMD Praxis der Wirtschaftsinformatik, pp. 1-21 (2023).
17. Heuer, M., Kurtz, C., Böhmann, T.: Towards a governance of low-code development platforms using the example of microsoft powerplatform in a multinational company. In: Proceedings of the 55th Hawaii International Conference on System Sciences, pp. 6881-6889, AISeL (2022).

18. Rokis, K., Kirikova, M.: Challenges of low-code/no-code software development: A literature review. In: International Conference on Business Informatics Research, pp. 3-17, Springer, Cham (2022).

19. vom Brocke, J., Simons, A., Niehaves, B., Riemer, K., Plattfaut, R., Cleven, A.: Reconstructing the Giang: On the Importance of Rigour in Documenting the Literature Search Process. In: Proceedings of the 17th European Conference on Information Systems (ECIS), AISeL (2009).

20. Webster, J., Watson, R.T.: Analyzing the Past to Prepare for the Future: Writing a Literature Review. MIS Quarterly xiii-xxiii (2002).

21. Cooper, H. M.: Organizing knowledge syntheses: A taxonomy of literature reviews. Knowledge in society, 1(1), 104-126 (1988).

22. Bandara, W., Furtmueller, E., Gorbacheva, E., Miskon, S., & Beekhuyzen, J.:. Achieving rigor in literature reviews: Insights from qualitative data analysis and tool-support. Communications of the Association for Information Systems, 37(1), 8, 154-204 (2015).

23. Rafiq, U., Filippo, C., Wang, X.: Understanding Low-Code or No-Code Adoption in Software Startups: Preliminary Results from a Comparative Case Study. In: Proceedings of the International Conference on Product-Focused Software Process Improvement (profess), pp. 390-398, Springer International Publishing, Cham (2022).

24. Li, M. M., Peters, C., Poser, M., Eilers, K., Elshan, E.: ICT-enabled job crafting: How Business Unit Developers use Low-code Development Platforms to craft jobs. In: Proceedings of the International Conference on Information Systems (ICIS), AISeL (2022).

25. Adrian, B., Hinrichsen, S., Schulz, A. and Voß, E.: Low-Code-Programmierungals Ansatz zur Gestaltung bedarfsgerechter informatorischer Assistenzsysteme – eine Fallstudie. In: Informatorische Assistenzsysteme in der variantenreichen Montage: Theorie und Praxis. pp. 173-186 (2020).

26. Sufi, F.: Algorithms in Low-Code-No-Code for Research Applications: A Practical Review. Algorithms 16.2, 108 (2023).

27. El Kamouchi, H., Kissi, M., El Beggar, O.: Low-code/No-code Development: A systematic literature review. In: Proceedings of the International Conference on Intelligent Systems: Theories and Applications (SITA), pp. 1-8, IEEE (2023).

28. Käss, S., Strahringer, S. and Westner, M.: Drivers and Inhibitors of Low Code Development Platform Adoption. In: Proceedings of the International Conference on Business Informatics (CBI), pp. 196-205 (2022).

29. Prinz, N., Huber, M., Riedinger, C., Rentrop, C.: Two Perspectives of Low-Code Development Platform Challenges – An Exploratory Study. In: Proceedings of the Pacific Asia Conference on Information Systems (PACIS), pp. 1-13, AISeL (2022).

30. Yan, Z.: The Impacts of Low/No-Code Development on Digital Transformation and Software Development. arXiv preprint arXiv:2112.14073 (2021).

31. Naqvi, S. A. A., Zimmer M. P., Syed, R., Drews, P.: Understanding the Socio-Technical Aspects of Low-Code Adoption for Software Development. In: Proceedings of the European Conference on Information Systems (ECIS), AISeL (2023).

32. Ward, J. M., & Griffiths, P. M.: Strategic planning for information systems. John Wiley & Sons, Inc., United States (1996).

33. Williams, J. J., Ramaprasad, A.: A taxonomy of critical success factors. European Journal of Information Systems, 5(4), 250-260 (1996).

Developing a VR Solution to Enhance Physical Learning

Dominic Jungmann[1]

[1] Reutlingen University, Reutlingen, Germany
Dominic.Jungmann@student.reutlingen-university.de

Abstract. Many of the traditional training methods are challenged by high failure rates and are neither as effective nor as efficient as desired. This research proposes a solution using virtual reality (VR) and digital twin technology to improve training effectiveness and engagement. By creating digital twins in form of three-dimensional (3D) scans of real-world objects and integrating them into a VR environment with A-Frame and the WebXR framework on the Meta Quest 3, trainees can interact with these objects in a realistic, immersive environment. The resulting minimum viable product (MVP) demonstrates an approach to virtual training by creating an environment including vehicles that can be opened to study their contents in detail and to find hidden objects. The MVP will be developed using scans from several vehicles at a local airport, with the goal of enhancing the training of airport security personnel with a solution that can be applied to a wider range of use cases. Key findings include scalable training scenarios that augment physical trainings with a virtual component, increasing training effectiveness, thus resulting in better trained personnel and improved efficiency.

Zusammenfassung. Hohe Fehlerquoten stellen eine Herausforderung für viele herkömmliche Trainingsmethoden dar. Mit Hilfe von Virtual Reality (VR) und digitalen Zwillingen soll in dieser Arbeit eine Grundlage geschaffen werden, welche die Trainingseffizienz und das -engagement steigert. Dazu werden digitale Zwillinge – in Form von dreidimensionalen (3D) Scans realer Objekte – geschaffen und mit den Frameworks A-Frame und WebXR in eine VR-Umgebung auf der Meta Quest 3 eingebunden, die Trainierenden die Möglichkeit einer direkten und interaktiven Interaktion in einer immersiven Umgebung ermöglicht. Das daraus resultierende Minimum Viable Product (MVP) stellt eine Umgebung mit Fahrzeugen dar, die geöffnet werden können, um ihren Inhalt im Detail zu begutachten, zu erlernen und versteckte Objekte zu finden. Dieses MVP wird auf der Grundlage von 3D-Scans von Fahrzeugen an einem lokalen Flughafen erschaffen und hat zum Ziel, das Training von Sicherheitspersonal zu verbessern, gleichzeitig aber auch eine Grundlage für Trainings in anderen Fachbereichen zu bieten.

© Der/die Autor(en), exklusiv lizenziert an
Springer Fachmedien Wiesbaden GmbH, ein Teil von Springer Nature 2025
M. Möhring et al. (Hrsg.), *Herman Hollerith Conference 2024*, Informatik aktuell,
https://doi.org/10.1007/978-3-658-48215-2_9

Zentrale Erkenntnisse umfassen skalierbare Trainingsszenarien, die physisches Training um eine virtuelle Komponente erweitern, die die Wirksamkeit des Trainings erhöht und somit besser ausgebildetes Personal und eine höhere Effizienz gewährleisten.

Keywords: Virtual Reality Training, Immersive Training, A-Frame, WebXR, Digital Twin, Enhancement of Physical Training by VR, Meta Quest.

1   Introduction

Ensuring the safety and security of an airport is a complex task, that relies mostly on the skills of airport security personnel [1,2,3]. Following Yin's case study methodology, specifically the multiple-case study approach [4], this paper examines the current methods of training in different departments at a regional airport in Germany with an annual passenger volume of 5 to 10 million. Recently, the airport has been increasing its focus on training and development, with some security personnel taking extra time to study, train and improve their skills for their mandatory employment tests. During these tests, participants are required to locate concealed objects, such as those hidden in vehicles. The increase in learning time indicates that the traditional training methods in use for these tests may be flawed. A similar situation faced by the airport can be found in the fire department, where personnel must learn and memorize the location of objects within equipment halls and vehicles by physically visiting them or from static images, which is not only inefficient, but also lacks the spatial representation necessary for emergencies. Additionally, the current training methods have one other issue: new employees of this department are given a guided tour of the buildings, which requires an extensive number of hours – equivalent to approximately one full workweek per new employee. In this topic, VR offers a revolutionizing potential for the creation of new training methods involving immersive, interactive, and thus realistic environments using digital twins.

The Objective of this research is to create an intuitive VR training world with 3D scans, interactions, and deployment on Meta Quest 3. Moreover, users should be able to move freely as they would in the real world. To achieve these goals, a straightforward and replicable process will be developed, resulting in the creation of a user-friendly MVP that will be usable at the end of this work, so it can support a positive training journey. The term MVP is used to describe a product with minimal functionality, and therefore minimal effort, that can be trialed with customers to gain feedback for future development [5].

This gives rise to the following **Research Questions**, which will be addressed in the present paper:

How can a 3D world be created by using digital twins of real-world objects?
How can this 3D world then be transformed into an interactive experience on the Meta Quest 3 that allows the user to freely move and interact with objects?

By answering these questions, this research aims to bridge the chasm between current training limitations and the potential of VR-enhanced training methods, unfolding an innovative solution for the training of airport security personnel. The results will not only improve the status quo of the addressed training, but also lay the groundwork for a broader application of VR training in future safety and security contexts. The corresponding source code is available at GitHub [6].

2   Background and Related Work

The following paragraphs will examine the fundamental technologies that are required for the work presented in this paper.

Digital Twin Technology. The "digital twin" technology enables real-time monitoring, diagnostics and simulation through virtual representations of physical objects [7,8]. These benefits are being realized in a wide range of industries, from traditional manufacturing to smart cities and urban planning to healthcare and aerospace, making it a prominent technology [7,8,9].

In this work, an excerpt of the digital twin is utilized solely for the purpose of simulating real-world behavior, without the goal of any additional enhancements.

Virtual Reality Training. The advent of VR has had a massive impact on training and education, enabling the completion of these activities in an immersive and interactive environment [10,11]. This leads to several benefits, including increased engagement [12], reduced risk during practice, improved observation skills and the ability to simulate complex and challenging scenarios [11,13]. Several studies have demonstrated that VR training can result in a more effective preservation of knowledge, a better acquisition of skills and overall training effectiveness compared to traditional methods [11,14]. It can even result in corresponding biometrics (e.g. heart rate, stress) as in real-world training [15].

Relevant Case Studies. Several case studies have highlighted the efficacy and applicability of VR-based trainings. For instance, Smith and Ericson [14] described an approach to teaching children the dangers of fire, potential fire hazards and escape routes. They conducted pre- and post-training assessments of the children's skills and identified a significant improvement. Another approach was developed by Haller et al. [16] approximately 25 years ago with an early-state VR training. The goal was to develop a training tool for a refinery, which led to the conclusion that VR training is highly practicable for teaching movement sequences, risky situations and situations that are difficult to build in real life.

Furthermore, recent research [13] highlights the potential of this topic including augmented reality (AR), mixed reality (MR) and VR in medical training for complex procedures such as hip replacement. A systematic review conducted by Su et al. [13] suggests that this new training method improves the accuracy of implant placement and shortens surgical time compared to conventional methods, giving a new scenario for VR training to enhance real world training with limited risks.

A study conducted by Kleygrewe et al. within the Dutch police force [15] evaluated the use of VR training in addition to real-world training. It found that VR training produced comparable psychological reactions, such as perceived stress and mental effort, despite lower bodily reactions (e.g. heart rate). In addition, VR offers the opportunity for flexibility in training environments without the need for real-world resources and provides efficient post-scenario evaluations.

Meta Quest, A-Frame and its Underlying Technologies. The Meta Quest, formerly known as the Oculus Quest, is a popular VR headset that offers a range of features, including hand tracking, spatial audio, and a wide field of view, making it suitable for immersive experiences [17] such as the training application that will be developed in this paper.

The Meta Quest platform is fully supported by A-Frame [18], a framework for building cross-platform experiences in VR and AR compatible with a wide range of devices [19] that comes with a 3D-Inspector, like the browser's developer tools with highly increased capabilities [20]. A-Frame combines several technologies [19]: WebGL to render 3D models in the web browser, WebXR to ensure that 3D scenes are rendered at optimal frame rates and to build motion vectors based on input devices [19,21] as well as Three.js, which is responsible for creating and rendering 3D scenes. HTTPS is mandatory to use WebXR [22]. It can be said that A-Frame plays the role of managing the different layers mentioned above, providing a platform to build VR/AR applications across different devices and simplifying the creation of immersive experiences with an HTML syntax, enhanced by CSS and JavaScript, making it easily accessible to developers and reducing the complexity of the different layers described previously [19].

The seamless integration of digital twins into the VR environment is enabled by this framework, making the development of interactive and realistic experiences possible.

3   Framework Development

This section describes the requirements for development, the creation of the digital twins and the setup of the environment as well as the subsequent programming in HTML   and   JavaScript.   The   source   code   is   available   at https://github.com/DominicJ7/VR-Training.

3.1   Requirements

This section provides an overview of the components necessary to address the research questions in a client-server approach and how these components are utilized during development. Based on an assessment of possible options for development and interviews with imaginable users, the requirements have been evaluated as shown in Table 1. The left side of the table outlines key objectives, while the right side presents corresponding solutions to meet these requirements, that will be discussed in the following.

Table 1. Requirements and proposed solutions.

Objective	Proposed Solution
User-friendly interface	Web-based or mobile app
Simplified development process	Web-based app
Acquisition of 3D models of airport vehicles	Utilization of iPad's LiDAR sensor
Interactions with 3D models: • Display a closed fire truck (after startup) • Open-button to open the truck • Close-button to close the truck • Reset-button to reset the scene • Two hidden objects inside the truck's compartment, collectable by the trainee	Web-based or mobile app
Cost-effective VR device	Meta Quest 3 headset

A web approach (see Fig. 1) is being employed as a straightforward initial method that can be easily adapted. Creating real (mobile) apps requires a Meta development account containing a self-written privacy policy, a responsible privacy officer, and is subject to restrictions regarding the number of created apps and the layout [22].

Firstly, 3D images will be taken using a specialized camera (the specifics of which will be outlined in the following paragraph). These files are then stored as glb-files in the root directories "assets", the former serves as the foundation of the website and contains the HTML too. The directory can be located either in a cloud storage (cloud approach) or on a local machine (local approach). The first approach will utilize a web-based development environment, while the second approach will use a local development environment as well as a local server. The application will then be accessed wearing the Meta Quest 3 (the device present at the researched airport for testing purposes). As previously mentioned, this requires an HTTPS connection to the server [21], making an SSL certificate mandatory for both the cloud and the local approach.

Fig. 1. Schematic representation of communication and data paths.

3.2   Creating Three-Dimensional Images/Digital Twins

To create 3D images, scientifically referred to as the digital twin of real-world ob-jects in this paper, the application "Polycam" [23] will be used. This application utilizes the iPad Pro's Light Detection and Ranging (LiDAR) sensor, which employs laser technology to determine distances to generate 3D scans of objects that contain spatial data. These objects can then be exported to a range of file formats [23] for utilization in this work.

3.3   Development

As explained in a previous section of this work, A-Frame can be used directly with the Meta Quest [18]. The approach of setting up the complete environment within this framework, considering all the necessary dependencies, will be described step by step in this part, followed by an explanation of the most important source code components.

Setting Up the Environment. Following the above explanation, the entire environ-ment will be built both cloud-based and locally installed. Both approaches can be used with the source code that will be explained later. The local approach will be used additionally, as it provides a better performance in the submission of changes, as well as better code editing features like code completion and keeping the code and assets locally, creating a better level of security for sensitive information.

Cloud Approach. To develop the prototype directly in the cloud, Glitch.com is being used. It is an online editor built for the creation of web applications. Additionally, it provides a live preview/editor [24], making it particularly useful for prototyping VR and AR projects. In this work, it is used exclusively to build the virtual environment by positioning, sizing and rotating all virtual objects in A-Frames Visual Inspector [20] and copying the resulting parameters into the code.

Local Approach. This approach uses a local machine running macOS. The develop-ment is accomplished using Visual Studio Code, running a local server with the Live Server extension [25] that can be accessed by the Meta Quest. This approach lacks one essential component: the SSL certificate needed to establish HTTPS, which is necessary for WebXR. A required certificate can be generated using mkcert, a tool for creating locally trusted development certificates. Running these prompts (see Code 1) in the macOS' Terminal will install it using homebrew and create the necessary certificates [26]:

```
% brew install mkcert #installs mkcert using Homebrew
% mkcert -key-file ~/key.pem -cert-file ~/cert.pem
  -install localhost 127.0.0.1 #creates key and certifi-
  cate, returns path to both files
```

Code 1. Installation of mkcert, creation of key and SSL-certificate.

This certificate can then be enabled in the Live Server by adding the following configuration (see Code 2) as settings.json in the parent root directory folder .vscode [27].

```
"liveServer.settings.https": {
    "enable": false,        //true to enable the feature
    "cert": ".../cert.pem", //path to SSL-certificate
    "key": ".../key.pem ",  //path to SSL-key },
```

Code 2. Settings in Live Server.

Creating the WebApp. As already discussed theoretically, the web application is created using HTML with A-Frame. Both the HTML-code, which forms the basic structure of the application, as well as the JavaScript-code, which allows interaction with the object, will now be described separately with snippets. The prototype should be able to do the following: display a closed fire truck, display an open-button (opening the truck), as well as a close-button for the opposite and a reset-button to reset the whole scene. In addition, two objects should be hidden inside the truck's compartment, e.g., a bottle of water and an avocado. These objects should then be collectable by the user.

Object Integration in HTML. Code 3 depicts the integration of an object in A-Frame. The A-Frame library is included in a script tag in the head section of the HTML, allowing the use of A-Frame components and entities within the body of the document. Inside the body, an A-Frame scene (<a-scene>) is defined, which serves as a container for all later VR elements. The scene includes following elements: a ground plane (<a-plane>) and a sky (<a-sky>) to define the environment as well as models of an open and closed fire truck, a water bottle, and an avocado. These objects are preloaded using (<a-asset-item>) in (<a-assets>). For example, the closed fire truck model is loaded as follows, adding a unique ID and the path to the corresponding asset and then integrated in the scene with a specific position, rotation, and visibility using the <a-entity> attribute containing the ID assigned in the previous part.

```
<a-assets>
<a-asset-item id="closedTruck" src="/Assets/Truck_closed.glb"></a-asset-item>
</a-assets>

<a-entity id="closedTruckModel"
  gltf-model="#closedTruck"
  position="1.121 1.779 -3.6"
  rotation="0 44.4 0"
  visible="true">
</a-entity>
```

Code 3. Basic object integration in A-Frame with HTML.

Code 4 describes the integration of controls. To allow the user to point and click on the desired elements, the right VR controller is integrated into the scene in an <a-entity>, containing the attributes ID, laser-controls (describing which side to use: left/right) and raycaster (specifying that all objects having the custom class "clickable" added to their <a-entity> can be interacted with).

```
<a-entity
  id="right-hand"
  laser-controls="hand: right"
  raycaster="objects: .clickable">
</a-entity>
```

Code 4. VR Controller in A-Frame with HTML.

Interactions in JavaScript. Code 5 is dedicated to bringing the environment to life. JavaScript is utilized to handle interactions with the VR environment and is placed in the HTML's <script>. The AFRAME.registerComponent contained therein is used to create an event listener for clicks on the button, calling the function openVehicle. The next section attaches the listener to the HTML's <a-entity> by using the document.querySelector to manipulate the properties of the corresponding entity, extending the "openButton" by the attribute "openbuttonlistener".

```
AFRAME.registerComponent("openbuttonlistener", {
  init: function () {
    var el = this.el;
    el.addEventListener("click", function () {
      openVehicle();
    }); }, });

document.querySelector("#openButton")
.setAttribute("openbuttonlistener", "");
```

Code 5. Interactions with JavaScript and A-Frame.

Additionally, various custom functions are defined to animate and reset the position, rotation and visibility of objects, making interactions possible and creating the (simple) illusion of opening and closing the doors of vehicles. All of these functions make use of the document.querySelector to manipulate the properties of each object.

4   Results and Discussion

The purpose of this section is to highlight the features of the MVP developed in the previous section, as well as the benefits and challenges of using this training method. It will also explain how future results could be evaluated.

Fig. 2 shows the MVP as seen in the Meta Quest. The left image depicts the closed fire truck, with the right controller clicking the "open" button, resulting in the middle image with the controller pointing at the bottle of water. Clicking on the bottle results in the right image, with the bottle collected and placed in front of the trainee and the black text label indicating that one of the two objects has been collected.

Fig. 2. Screenshots from the Meta Quest: three different situations in the VR-environment.

Fig. 3 presents a subsequent iteration of the MVP, featuring a model of an airplane simulator. The images were captured in the same way as above. Within this model, users can navigate freely or use designated green buttons to quickly move between different positions. Clicking the blue button results in the opening of the cockpit door. Since the core code structure remains unchanged, and for the purpose of simplicity, the code specifics will not be explained further. As previously, the movement of objects and the opening and closing of doors are created by blending in and out the appropriate images. For example, this scan includes a serving cart that can be pulled out of its housing by clicking the corresponding button.

Fig. 3. Screenshots from the Meta Quest: the next iteration of the MVP.

Benefits of using this Method of Training. The process of development and the testing of the MVP has continued to demonstrate the advantages of the approach for the construction of a virtual environment for training in challenging and resource-intensive environments, as outlined in reference papers. The training method can be used independently, without the necessity for a trainer or a dedicated training environment, even for short periods. Moreover, it can be used with an unlimited number of training environments and objects, whereas these factors are limited in the current analog methods of training. Finally, gamification can lead to an enhanced engagement of the trainee, leading to better results.

Challenges and Limitations. One of the most demanding challenges during the building of the MVP was the generation of 3D objects. While the use of an iPad's LiDAR scanner was an efficient method for the initial generation of the models, this approach does not provide the requisite graphical quality for further developments. Another issue arises with the creation of the virtual environment. Each object must be integrated and placed manually, as well as programmed for potential actions. Finally, the costs of VR headsets (in this case, Meta Quests) and hosting the website must be considered. These costs must be weighed against the potential savings from replacing or enhancing real training.

Testing. Future testing of a more advanced version of the MVP could evaluate results for effectiveness and efficiency, two fundamental measures when comparing different processes [28].

Effectiveness. This measure describes the level to which the result is archived [28,29]. Regarding the context of this MVP, it gauges how the result of virtual training compares to the result of previous traditional training methods.

The comparison of the effectiveness of the new training approach vs. the traditional training should include the following measures to directly compare the results of both: the extension of knowledge acquisition (to which degree the number of remembered objects and their location by the trainee increases), the ability of applying learned skills in both scenarios (how many objects can the trainee find) and finally the long-term preservation of both methods after a specific period of time.

Efficiency. This measure describes the ratio of how many input resources are needed to archive the desired outcome [28,29]. Regarding the context of this MVP, it evaluates how VR training compares to previous traditional training methods in terms of human resources, time and money.

The comparison of these two approaches should be archived by considering the costs of both, including the time required for participants and instructors/trainers, the resources required (classrooms, Meta Quest, servers, scans and software) and subsequently the money required to archive the same result.

5 Conclusion and Future Work

This work has successfully demonstrated how digital twins created from scans of real-world objects can be used to create interactive, immersive training environments to enhance traditional training methods and the engagement of trainees. The associated development of the MVP has shown significant potential in addressing the current limitations of traditional training methods at the local airport.

By developing a replicable method for building similar products, this approach answered the two research questions:

To start, the different methods of creating digital twins of real-world objects (e.g., using an iPad's LiDAR sensor) and transferring them into a virtual 3D world were explained and evaluated, thus answering the first research question.

The second objective involved exploring how this 3D world could be transformed into an interactive experience, allowing the user to freely move and interact with objects, thereby addressing the second research question. This was accomplished by creating an environment in A-Frame that integrates the above objects, Meta Quest controls and JavaScript to handle all necessary interactions.

In the future, a new iteration of the MVP should be developed, that could demonstrate several key benefits, including enhanced effectiveness and engagement in training, independence from physical trainers and environments, scalable training scenarios, gamification elements and cost reduction. However, several challenges remain to be addressed, including the graphical quality of the objects and their manual integration, as well as the costs associated with VR equipment and hosting. Graphical quality seems to be the biggest issue with this MVP. Initial tests have shown that the quality of the images from the iPad's built-in LiDAR sensor is not sufficient for real-world training environments. Nevertheless, it is a quick and inexpensive way to see initial results.

As one can see, only a first MVP has been built in this work. Therefore, no specific results can be given now. Future work will concentrate on enhancing the quality of digital twins by employing more advanced scanning technology and expanding the range of possible interactions, thereby increasing the realism and effectiveness of the training scenarios. Additionally, the product will be tested in different types of real training scenarios to evaluate its impact on training quality and results, regarding both the effectiveness and the efficiency of this product. By continuously improving the models, interactions and training exercises, this solution can then be used in multiple training contexts, resulting in better trained personnel and improved operational efficiency.

References

1. Frederickson, H., LaPorte, T. Airport security, high reliability, and the problem of rational Public Administration Review, 62, 33-43 (2002).
2. Naji, M. et al. Airport security screening process: a review. 17th COTA International Conference of Transportation Professionals (pp. 3978-3988). Reston, VA: American Society of Civil Engineers (2017).

3. Hainmüller, J., Lemnitzer, J. Why do Europeans fly safer? The politics of airport security in Europe and the US. Terrorism and political violence, 15(4), 1-36 (2003).
4. Yin, R. Case study research and applications (2018).
5. Lenarduzzi, V., Taibi, D. MVP explained: A systematic mapping study on the definitions of minimal viable product. 42th Euromicro Conference on Software Engineering and Advanced Applications, 112-119 (2016).
6. Jungmann, D. VR-Training, https://github.com/DominicJ7/VR-Training, last accessed 2024/10/29.
7. Glaessgen, E., Stargel, D. The digital twin paradigm for future NASA and U.S. air force vehicles. 53rd Structures, Structural Dynamics, and Materials Conference: Special Session on the Digital Twin (2012).
8. Tao, F. et al. Digital twin-driven product design, manufacturing and service with big data. The International Journal of Advanced Manufacturing Technology 94, 3563–3576 (2018).
9. Xia, H. et al. Study on city digital twin technologies for sustainable smart city design: A review and bibliometric analysis of geographic information system and building information modeling integration. Sustainable Cities and Society, 84, 10400 (2022).
10. Bharathi, A., Tucker, C. Investigating the impact of interactive immersive virtual reality environments in enhancing task performance in online engineering design activities. International Design Engineering Technical Conferences and Computers and Information in Engineering Conference (Vol. 57106, p. V003T04A004). American Society of Mechanical Engineers (2015).
11. Jensen, L., Konradsen, F. A review of the use of virtual reality head-mounted displays in education and training. Education and Information Technologies 23, 1515–1529 (2018).
12. Pruemmer, J., van Steen, T., van den Berg, B. A systematic review of current cybersecurity training methods. Computers & Security, 103585 (2023).
13. Su, S. et al. The effectiveness of virtual reality, augmented reality, and mixed reality training in total hip arthroplasty: a systematic review and meta-analysis. Journal of Orthopaedic Surgery and Research, 18(1), 121 (2023).
14. Smith, S., Ericson, E. Using immersive game-based virtual reality to teach fire-safety skills to children. Virtual Reality 13, 87–99 (2009).
15. Kleygrewe, L., et al. Virtual reality training for police officers: A comparison of training responses in VR and real-life training. Police Practice and Research, 25(1), 18-37 (2024).
16. Haller, M. et al. omVR—a safety training system for a virtual refinery (1999).
17. Meta Platforms, Inc. Meta Homepage - Expand your world with Meta Quest, https://www.meta.com/de/quest, last accessed 2024/06/06.
18. Marcos, D. Releases/v.1.5.0., https://github.com/aframevr/aframe/releases/tag/v1.5.0, last accessed 2024/11/04.
19. Macario, G. WebXR, A-Frame and Networked-Aframe as a Basis for an Open Metaverse: A Conceptual Architecture (2024).
20. A-Frame. Visual Inspector & Dev Tools, https://aframe.io/docs/1.6.0/introduction/visual-inspector-and-dev-tools.html, last accessed 2024/11/09.
21. W3C. WebXR Device API, https://immersive-web.github.io/webxr, last accessed 2024/06/06.
22. Meta Platforms, Inc. Create an App, https://developers.facebook.com/docs/development/create-an-app, last accessed 2024/06/07.
23. Polycam. 3D LIDAR SCANNER & RECONSTRUCTION TOOL, https://poly.cam/tools/3d-lidar-scanner, last accessed 2024/06/07.

24. Glitch. Build your new reality on Glitch, https://glitch.com/webxr, last accessed 2024/06/08.
25. Dey, R. Live Server, https://marketplace.visualstudio.com/items?itemName=ritwick-dey.
    LiveServer, last accessed 2024/06/08.
26. Valsorda, F. mkcert, https://github.com/FiloSottile/mkcert, last accessed 2024/06/08.
27. Dey, R. Settings, https://github.com/ritwickdey/vscode-live-server/blob/HEAD/docs/settings.md, last accessed 2024/06/08.
28. Sundqvist, E., Backlund, F., Chronéer, D. What is project efficiency and effectiveness?. Procedia-Social and Behavioral Sciences, 119, 278-287 (2014).
29. Zidane, Y., Olsson, N. Defining project efficiency, effectiveness and efficacy. International Journal of Managing Projects in Business, 10(3), 621-641 (2017).

The potential of generative AI in value-based selling

Victoria Sauter[1]

[1] Herman Hollerith Zentrum, Danziger Straße 6, 71034 Böblingen, Germany
victoria-sauter@web.de

Abstract. Value-based selling, a highly customer-centric sales approach that emphasizes the delivery of tailored value propositions, aims to establish long-term customer relationships and impact customers' business goals. This research explores the potential of generative AI (genAI), as a rising technology of artificial intelligence, to enhance value-based selling by offering new opportunities for efficiency and effectiveness. By identifying and analyzing several use cases, this study shows how genAI can drive significant improvements in faster, more comprehensive research, customer experience and loyalty. Key challenges of using genAI in value-based selling include managing data quality and availability as well as personnel aspects. One prominent use case, customer insight generation, has been validated through a detailed preliminary experiment, confirming its practical value in real-world scenarios. To fully leverage genAI in value-based selling, recommendations are to drive the adoption of genAI with a clear strategy, prioritize data availability and quality, focus on valuable use cases, effective sales communication, and enablement, and establish clear policies and guidelines for the responsible use of genAI.

Zusammenfassung. Value-based Selling ist ein stark kundenorientierter Verkaufsansatz, der sich auf die Bereitstellung maßgeschneiderter Wertangebote konzentriert und darauf abzielt, langfristige Kundenbeziehungen aufzubauen und die Geschäftsziele der Kunden zu beeinflussen. Dieses Paper untersucht das Potenzial der generativen KI (genAI), einer aufkommenden Technologie der künstlichen Intelligenz, den wertorientierten Vertrieb durch neue Möglichkeiten der Effizienz und Effektivität zu verbessern. Durch die Identifizierung und Analyse verschiedener Anwendungsfälle zeigt diese Studie, wie genAI signifikante Verbesserungen in der schnelleren und umfassenderen Suche, Kundenerfahrung und Kundenbindung ermöglicht. Die wichtigsten Herausforderungen beim Einsatz von genAI im wertorientierten Vertrieb sind das Management der Datenqualität und -verfügbarkeit sowie Personalaspekte.

© Der/die Autor(en), exklusiv lizenziert an
Springer Fachmedien Wiesbaden GmbH, ein Teil von Springer Nature 2025
M. Möhring et al. (Hrsg.), *Herman Hollerith Conference 2024*, Informatik aktuell,
https://doi.org/10.1007/978-3-658-48215-2_10

Ein prominenter Anwendungsfall, die Generierung von Customer Insights, wurde durch ein detailliertes Pre-Experiment validiert, das den praktischen Nutzen in realen Szenarien bestätigt. Um die Vorteile von genAI im wertorientierten Vertrieb voll auszuschöpfen, wird empfohlen, die Einführung von genAI mit einer klaren Strategie voranzutreiben, Datenverfügbarkeit und - qualität zu priorisieren, sich auf wertvolle Anwendungsfälle, effektive Kommunikation und Befähigung zu konzentrieren und klare Richtlinien für den verantwortungsvollen Einsatz von genAI zu definieren.

Keywords: generative AI, Value-based selling, AI for businesses, Literature Review, Experiment.

1   Introduction

The change from product-led selling to customer-centric sales approaches has been prominent in the last decade [1]. This transformation is particularly evident in the adoption of value-based selling (VBS), which focuses on establishing meaningful relationships and delivering value to customers [2]. VBS prioritizes comprehending and addressing each customer's distinctive needs and objectives, aiming to foster long-term partnerships rather than one-time transactions [3].

On the other hand, the emerging trend of Artificial Intelligence (AI) is also disrupting how organizations drive their operational businesses [4]. Gartner predicts that *"by 2026, over 100 million humans will engage robocolleagues to contribute to their work"* [5]. Supportive of this assumption is the rise of generative AI (genAI), a subfield of AI enabling original content generation. Since the launch of ChatGPT by OpenAI in 2022, *"businesses are racing to capture its value"* [6]. As genAI continues to advance, its influence on business practices will likely reshape the landscape of operational efficiency and strategic decision-making.

The approach of VBS is inherently time-consuming and heavily data-driven, demanding that sales professionals gather, analyze, and apply extensive customer insights to tailor their value propositions effectively [3]. This complexity can significantly hinder efficiency, particularly in business-to-business (B2B) sales environments with lengthy decision-making processes [7]. Concurrently, the incorporation of genAI into business processes has demonstrated considerable potential for enhancing efficiency and simplifying operations [5]. Therefore, this research aims to identify use cases for integrating genAI into VBS, focusing on the expected outcomes, key success factors, and potential challenges for each. Among these identified use cases, one will be selected for testing and validation through a structured preliminary experiment to assess the effectiveness of genAI in enhancing VBS. The ultimate goal is to develop actionable recommendations businesses can implement to integrate genAI into their VBS strategies successfully. To achieve these objectives, the following research questions will be addressed:

"What are the most promising use cases for integrating genAI into VBS, the key success factors and challenges together with recommendations of adoption, and how can businesses adopt genAI effectively?"

This paper is divided into four main sections. Following the introduction are the theoretical foundations of VBS and genAI as two focused objects. Thirdly, the first part of the research question, the potential usage of genAI in VBS, will be evaluated by applying the methodology of a systematic literature review (LR) supported by interviews with VBS practitioners. Validating the findings and preparing for the second part of the research questions, recommendations for adoption, one identified use case will be tested in a preliminary experiment. The paper concludes with a summary and outlook for further research.

2   Background and fundamentals

The research focuses on the potential of genAI in VBS. VBS, a highly value-driven and customer-centric sales approach, and genAI, a promising technology, are the key elements that will be covered in this section.

2.1   Value-based selling

VBS represents a sales strategy predicated on a customer-centric approach and the generation of customer value. The overarching objective of VBS is to assist the customer in achieving their strategic objectives, fulfilling their desired outcomes, and establishing a long-term customer relationship [3]. VBS is less concerned with presenting an offering to the customer; rather, it is focused on demonstrating the business impact that will increase the customer's profits [3].

At the core of VBS lies the concept of value. The value of a product can be defined as the ratio of the benefits it offers to the price paid for it [8]. The customer value encompasses the capabilities that enable the customer to achieve their business goals [9], and is therefore tailored to align with the customer's business aspirations [9]. The development of the value proposition necessitates a comprehensive understanding of the customer's business [9].

The process of VBS includes the aforementioned principles and the value in its definition and delivery. Within the literature, three different processes and approaches could be identified: Terho et. al. [2], Töytäri et. al. [3], Töytäri and Rajala [10]. The three frameworks present different approaches to the VBS process and emphasize different aspects of customer engagement. While Terho [2] focus on a three-step process of understanding the customer's business, creating a value proposition, and communicating it effectively, Töytäri et al. [3] present a more detailed, customer-specific eightstep approach emphasizing internal analysis and collaboration. Töytäri and Rajala [10] extend this idea into a three-phase programmatic framework that includes planning, implementation, and leveraging value through systematic documentation. Despite these differences, all three models emphasize the need for deep customer understanding and strategic value communication. The research considers the three approaches and aligns them into a four-stage and seven-step process (see **Fig. 1**).

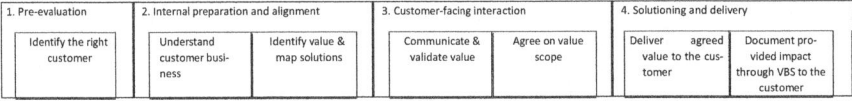

1. Pre-evaluation	2. Internal preparation and alignment		3. Customer-facing interaction		4. Solutioning and delivery	
Identify the right customer	Understand customer business	Identify value & map solutions	Communicate & validate value	Agree on value scope	Deliver agreed value to the customer	Document provided impact through VBS to the customer

Fig. 1. VBS process curated from existing approaches [3, 2, 10]

2.2 Generative AI

The concept of AI has evolved from a futuristic idea to a *"central component of modern technology"* [11], especially with the rise of ChatGPT, which has integrated AI into daily life [12]. AI encompasses research into machine intelligence, leading to several subcategories [13], with machine learning (ML) being the first. ML algorithms learn from data without explicit programming [13, 14], while deep learning employs neural networks to analyze data [13]. GenAI represents a significant advancement, generating new data by learning patterns from existing data [13, 5, 11]. It is considered a disruptive technology [15] but requires a human-centered approach for success, emphasizing empathy, transparency, and ethics [16]. The announcement of ChatGPT in 2022 marked a boom for genAI [6]. Beyond text generation, genAI can create images, audio, video, code, and other digital content, making it a versatile tool [13, 5, 11].

GenAI is a hot topic in business, with leaders pressured to adopt new technologies for competitive advantage [17, 18], making it a priority in boardrooms [19]. Gartner [5] identifies three opportunity categories for genAI: revenue, cost and productivity, and risk. GenAI accelerates product development, boosts efficiency through rapid content and code generation, and helps detect risks while ensuring regulatory compliance [5]. However, current use cases mainly focus on productivity over innovation [17].

Despite its potential, genAI poses risks and challenges in business, ethics, regulation, and technology. Companies struggle to balance AI's benefits with the need for control, and trust is often limited due to issues like data quality and hallucinations [17]. Concerns about data security arise, especially with tools such as ChatGPT, which risk exposing internal data [19]. Ethical challenges include biased outputs and fake content, which undermine trust [16]. Ensuring data quality and preventing AI hallucinations are critical for reliability [16].

In summary it is important to address challenges in the evaluation of a genAI approach in order to unlock the potential.

3   Usage of genAI in Value-based selling

This paper aims to identify promising use cases for genAI in VBS. The approach is structured into four steps. First, data collection is conducted to highlight existing research and application on genAI applications which will then be integrated and mapped onto the process of VBS. For data evaluation a preliminary experiment tests the practical implementation of one identified use case. All findings result in recommendations for business to adopt genAI in VBS.

3.1   Data collection

First, a LR is conducted to establish a theoretical foundation and highlight existing research on genAI applications in sales. Next, in-depth interviews with practitioners will be conducted to gather practical insights, which will then be integrated and mapped onto the process of VBS.

Literature review. The process of the systematic LR, mainly the four parts defined by Cooper in 1984 [20], will be applied and enhanced by elements from Kitchenham and Charters [21], Kitchenham et. al [22], and Fink [23].

The first step, problem identification [24], includes defining the research purpose, inclusion and exclusion criteria, and search terms. The general problem statement of the research can also be seen as the problem statement for the systematic LR: Identifying the use cases of genAI in VBS as the merger of two significant trends. The inclusion and exclusion criteria support the process of publication qualification and provide guidelines [20, 22, 23]. Selected criteria are: year of publication (>2018); language (German or English); availability (institutional subscription or public); type (primary literature or secondary literature), sales type (B2B), technology (genAI), database (IEEE, ACM, Science Direct, Research Gate, DOAJ, Springer), Type (Journal, Book, Conference Paper). For the search term [21], potential components in the context have been identified: generative; AI; value-based; selling. By considering alternatives for the components, the search term: *[gen AND Artificial AND Intelligence AND Value Based AND selling]* was selected. Furthermore, a more generic alternative is applied: *[((Artificial AND Intelligence) OR AI) AND Sales].*

After identifying the problem, the next step involves documenting [21] and selecting publications for data collection [21]. The process is tracked in a spreadsheet detailing search terms, hits, scanned publications, and availability. Each search term is applied in different libraries. Non-academic but qualified publications based on the inclusion and exclusion criteria were also included. About 70% of pre-identified papers were excluded after full-text scanning due to irrelevant content. In total, 33 publications were selected for further evaluation.

After pre-selecting publications, the third step, data evaluation, begins [22]. This involves assessing the quality of the 33 publications against selection criteria, narrowing it down to 22 that focus on sales or genAI (see **Table 1**)

Table 1. Identified and qualified 22 publications for the literature review

Author	Title	Year	genAI
Rainsberger, Livia	AI - The new intelligence in sales	2022	x
Gartner	AI in Sales: The Secret to Closing More Deals | Gartner	2023	x
Deveau, Richelle; Griffin, Sonia Joseph; Reis, Steve	AI powered- Marketing and Sales reach new heights	2023	x
Moradi, Masoud; Dass, Mayukh	Applications of artificial intelligence in B2B marketing: Challenges and future directions	2022	x
Benbya, Hind; Davenport, Thomas H.; Pachidi, Stella	Artificial Intelligence in Organizations- Current Sata and Future Opportunities	2020	x
Unni, Manu Vasudevan; Rudresh, S.; Rashmi, Bh; Renjith Krishnan, K.; Kar, Rohit; Devichandrika, S.	Automation using Artificial Intelligence in Business Landscape	2023	x
Huang, Ken; Wang, Yang; Zhu, Feng; Chen, Xi; Xing, Chunxiao	Beyond AI	2023	x
Kumari, Sharda; Kumar, Vipin; Sharmila, A.; Murthy, C. Ravindra; Ahlawat, Navin; Manoharan, Geetha	Big Data and Artificial Intelligence Revolutionizing business decision making	2023	x
Paschen, Jeannette; Wilson, Matthew; Ferreira, João J.	Collaborative intelligence: How human and artificial intelligence create value along the B2B sales funnel	2020	x
Makar, Katarina Šiber	Driven by Artificial Intelligence (AI) – Improving Operational Efficiency and Competitiveness in Business	2023	x
Bhāle, Sanjay	Enhancing value proposition through AI strategy	2019	x
Seaton	Generative AI: 5 enterprise predictions for AI and security — for 2023, 2024, and beyond	2023	x

Thiruneelakandan, A.; Uma-mageswari, A.	Generative AI: A Transformative Force in Business Intelligence	2024	x
Engels, Robert; Tolido, Ron; Slatter, Marisa; a.o.	Harnessing the potential of genAI	2023	x
Sinha, Prabhakant; Shastri, Arun; Lorimer, Sally E.	How Generative AI Will Change Sales	2023	x
Bajaria, Viral	How To Maximize The Power Of Generative AI In Sales And Marketing	2023	x
Bode, Christoph; Bogasche-wsky, Ronald; Eßig, Mi-chael; Lasch, Rainer; Stölzle, Wolfgang	Supply Management Research	2022	x
Chui, Michael; Hazan, Eric; Roberts, Roger; a.o.	The economic potential of genera-tive AI	2023	x
Kunal; Rana, Muskaan; Bansal, Jatin	The Future of OpenAI Tools: Oppor-tunities and Challenges for Human-AI Collaboration	2023	x
Kanbach, Dominik K.; Hei-duk, Louisa; Blueher, Georg; Schreiter, Maximilian; Lah-mann, Alexander	The GenAI is out of the bottle: gen-erative artificial intelligence from a business model innovation perspec-tive	2024	x
Khalil, Faisal; Pipa, Gordon	Transforming the generative pre-trained transformer into aug-mented business text writer	2022	x
Kar, Arpan Kumar; Varsha, P. S.; Rajan, Shivakami	Unravelling the Impact of Genera-tive Artificial Intelligence (GAI) in In-dustrial Applications: A Review of Scientific and Grey Literature	2023	x

These 22 publications were read thoroughly, and relevant sections were inductively coded [24] using Mayring's methodology, a structured, rule-based approach de-signed for systematic analysis of qualitative data, allowing for flexible categoriza-tion and interpretation of medium-sized data sets [25–27]. Codes were grouped into four categories: use cases, challenges, benefits, and implementation. The final step is the evaluation of the findings (see 3.2).

Interviews. In addition to the systematic LR, n=5 interviews were conducted. Given the high relevance of this topic, insights directly from the field were valuable for crosschecking perspectives found in the literature. For the interviews, individu-als who had strategically developed the implementation of VBS and/or successfully implemented it for clients were selected. The interviews aimed to identify individuals' roles in the VBS process and their definitions, facilitating a comparison between theoretical and practical understandings. They also captured prior experiences with genAI tools, along with potential challenges and future visions for their use in VBS. The data collection interviews followed a guided approach, with participants receiving an interview guide containing narrative prompts, pre-formulated questions, and keywords for spontaneous inquiries [28]. After scheduling the interview via Teams and providing a briefing, the conversation will be recorded and transcribed verbatim for analysis, with a final review conducted to ensure clarity and usefulness [25, 29].

3.2   Data evaluation

The final stage in identifying genAI's potential in VBS involves synthesizing results by evaluating 22 publications (see 3.1) to identify use case groups, success factors, challenges, and outcomes, complemented by insights from practitioner interviews, with findings compared to the VBS process to assess applicability at each step. As the use cases identified in the LR are predominantly related to sales in general, the use cases were named more in the context of the respective VBS process steps (see **Fig. 2**). This step was informed by the VBS foundations and insights derived from the interviews with VBS practitioners. For instance, for Step 2, understanding the customer business, the initial assignment was the use cases market research and customer research. In theory, it became evident that this is a more far-reaching concept, with the information being interconnected to create a value proposition for the customer. The interviews also indicated that the information should be structured for enhanced presentation, resulting in three specific use cases: *customer insight generation, extracting and prioritizing information from external and internal data, and generating and aligning industry insights with customer initiatives.*

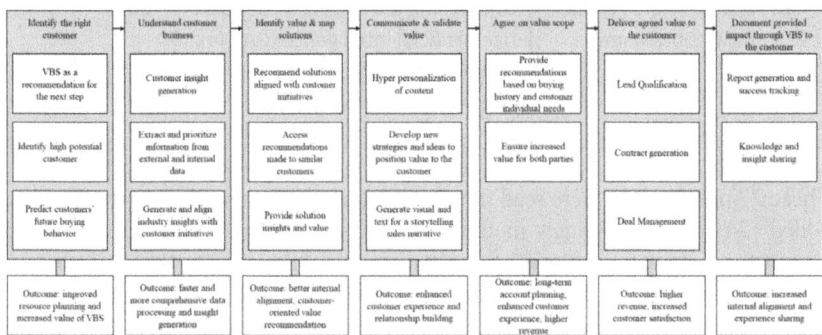

Fig. 2. Illustration of the findings of potential use case of genAI in VBS

Furthermore, success factors could be derived from the LR and the interviews as prerequisites or actions supporting the successful adoption of genAI (Sales enablement, human information validation, data availability, data management and accessibility). Contrary challenges highlight potential risks and barriers (Data quality, data availability, incorrect & biased output, timeliness of information, lack of inherent understanding).

3.3   Preliminary data validation

The previous step of identifying use cases for genAI in VBS was validated with a preliminary experiment exploring one of the use cases. The experiment is structured in three phases (see **Fig. 3**).

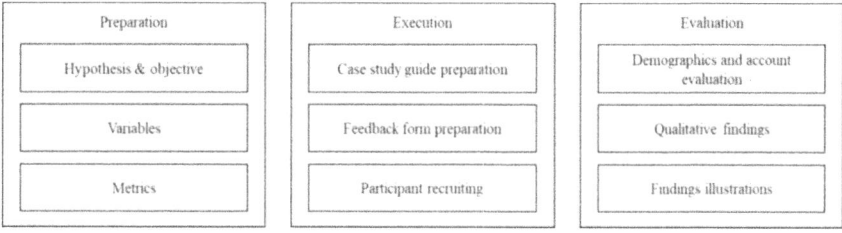

Fig. 3. Preliminary experiment process overview

In the preparation phase, the initial step involved defining the research hypotheses and objectives to guide the study's direction. The hypothesis H1 was stated as follows: *"The implementation of genAI has the potential to positively influence the second step of the VBS process, understanding customer business, by enhancing data gathering and customer insights generation despite existing challenges,"* with the chosen use case being Customer Insight Generation. Next, key variables to be measured and manipulated were identified. The independent variable measured was the genAI tool, Copilot by Microsoft, while the dependent variables included elements of customer research (business understanding, line of business insights, financial insights, and industry insights). The confounding variables comprised participants' research and genAI experience. Metrics to evaluate the study's results— efficiency, effectiveness, accuracy, and confidence of the research output—were then determined. Additionally, a detailed experiment guide and feedback form were developed to ensure consistent and thorough data collection.

The execution phase commenced with the recruitment of participants for the experiment. The author aimed for ten participants, divided into two groups of five: Group A, the control group, and Group B, the test group. To select suitable participants, the VBS program leads were consulted to nominate appropriate VBS practitioners. A total of n=16 people were identified and invited to participate in the experiment; of these, n=15 responded, and n=9 agreed to participate. Each participant chose which group to join, resulting in n=5 in Group A and n=4 in Group B. Group

A conducted the experiment without the influence of the independent variable, while Group B conducted it with the influence of Copilot. Finally, in the evaluation phase, the collected feedback forms were reviewed to gather qualitative insights, while pre-defined metrics were analyzed to quantify study results. The process concluded with a summary of findings that integrated qualitative feedback and quantitative data to draw comprehensive conclusions and make informed recommendations.

To assess genAI's impact, the feedback from Group A was contrasted with the outcomes in Group B. For efficiency, Group A required a minimum of three hours, while Group B was able to reduce the time to one to two hours with Copilot. This suggests that, if focusing solely on the time taken for customer research and insight generation, efficiency could indeed be increased. Although it was impossible to measure effectiveness directly regarding pipeline generation, it was postulated that a higher throughput rate and greater utilization of the VBS approach would result in more pipelines being generated. Group B agreed that deploying a genAI tool would increase their account throughput rate. Accuracy and confidence ratings were found to be similar across both groups, with variations primarily due to customer data availability. Both groups expressed satisfaction with accuracy and confidence levels, indicating that the same confidence could be achieved with reduced time and effort. This outcome of the preliminary experiment reflects positively on genAI's potential in enhancing VBS processes.

4   Recommendations for adoption

Based on the entire research and the discussion of the findings, the final step is to develop recommendations for adopting genAI in VBS. Four recommendations could be identified based on the previously discussed challenges and success factors to support the desired outcomes: Strategy (R1), Data (R2), Use cases (R3), and Sales enablement (R4). These recommendations are designed to provide additional support for successful adoption, ensuring that genAI is effectively utilized within the specific context of VBS operations. Moreover, they offer a structured approach to navigating the complexities of genAI adoption, helping businesses to harness its potential while mitigating associated risks. In the following, each theme will be transposed into a recommendation, its rationale, and orientational questions to approach the recommendations in a summary at the end (see **Fig. 4**).

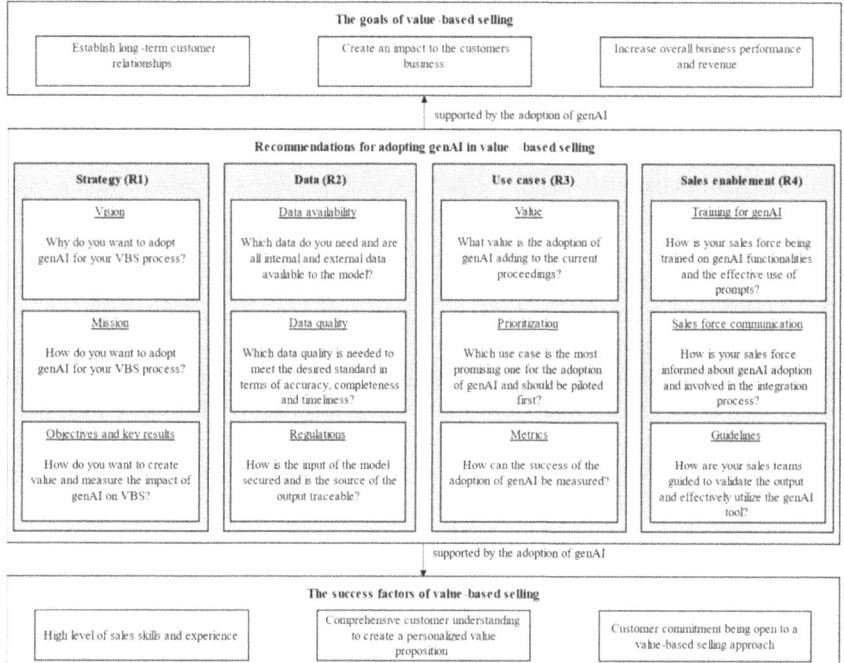

Fig. 4. Recommendations for the adoption of genAI in VBS

Strategy (R1): For effective genAI adoption in VBS, a strategic approach is essential. Beyond aligning with overall business goals, a tailored strategy specific to VBS processes is crucial. This should include a clear vision, mission, and preliminary objectives with measurable KPIs to ensure progress is trackable and aligned with business goals. **Data (R2):** Data accessibility is foundational, with a focus on both internal and external customer information as well as product data to support accurate value propositions. Effective integration of these data sources will determine tool selection and may require custom model training to reflect company values. Prioritizing data quality is critical, as accurate, unbiased data underpins customer insights and decision-making in VBS. **Use Cases (R3):** Identifying high-impact genAI use cases is essential for maximizing value, with initial pilots prioritized for measurable outcomes. GenAI's application should be context-specific, with consideration of data availability and the right tools for each use case. Flexibility in tool selection is advised, as some scenarios may require multiple or customized tools.

Sales Enablement (R4): Clear communication with the sales force is vital to convey genAI's supportive role, along with comprehensive training in genAI functionality and effective prompt use. Establishing guidelines for verifying genAI outputs through additional sources and peer consultation will enhance confidence, improve the accuracy of value propositions, and support the goal of fostering lasting customer relationships.

5   Conclusion and discussion

In summary, this research illustrates the potential of genAI to significantly enhance each stage of the VBS process, with essential success factors such as effective sales enablement, robust data management, and accessible information validation. While challenges like data quality, data bias, and timeliness of information remain obstacles, the integration of genAI shows promise in improving long-term planning, revenue generation, operational efficiency, and customer satisfaction. Specifically, the preliminary experiment on customer insight generation validated genAI's benefits in enhancing efficiency and effectiveness, demonstrating how tools like Copilot can streamline processes by quickly summarizing and contextualizing critical customer information. This paper proposes four primary recommendations for organizations adopting genAI in VBS: first, to develop a comprehensive genAI strategy aligned with business goals; second, to ensure accessible and high-quality data; third, to identify and prioritize highvalue genAI use cases; and fourth, to support sales teams with ongoing communication, clear guidelines, and tailored training to maximize effective use.

A critical reflection revealed certain limitations, including the restricted availability of genAI research within the VBS field and a small sample size of interviewees, predominantly from a single organization. Although these constraints impact the generalizability of findings, the study still contributes valuable insights, underscoring the importance of further exploration and testing across a more diverse and comprehensive sample. Future research should aim to validate additional use cases, integrate both internal and external data sources to enhance genAI's accuracy and applicability, and focus on the practical implementation of these recommendations. This will support businesses in developing actionable strategies to fully leverage genAI's transformative potential within VBS processes, ultimately enabling more informed decision-making, efficient sales processes, and enhanced customer engagement.

References

1. Ohiomah A, Benyoucef M, Andreev P (2020) A multidimensional perspective of business-to-business sales success: A meta-analytic review, University of Ottawa
2. Terho H, Haas A, Eggert A et al. (2012) It's almost like taking the sales out of sell-ing—Towards a conceptualization of value-based selling in business markets. Indus-trial Marketing Management 41:174–185. https://doi.org/10.1016/j.indmarman.2011.11.011
3. Töytäri P, Brashear Alejandro T, Parvinen P et al. (2011) Bridging the theory to application gap in value-based selling. Journal of Business & Industrial Marketing 26:493–502. https://doi.org/10.1108/08858621111162299
4. Chui M, Hazan E, Roberts R et al. (2023) The economic potential of generative AI: The next productivity frontier. https://www.mckinsey.de/~/media/mckinsey/locations/europe%20and%20middle%20east/deutschland/news/presse/2023/2023-06-

14%20mgi%20genai%20report%202023/the-economic-potential-of-generative-ai-the-next-productivity-frontier-vf.pdf. Accessed 13 Aug 2024

5. Gartner (2024) Generative AI: What Is It, Tools, Models, Applications and Use Cases. https://www.gartner.com/en/topics/generative-ai. Accessed 31 Mar 2024

6. McKinsey & Company (2023) What's the future of generative AI? An early view in 15 charts. https://www.mckinsey.com/featured-insights/mckinsey-explainers/whats-the-fu-ture-of-generative-ai-an-early-view-in-15-charts. Accessed 19 Aug 2024

7. Hess G (2022) Bust The Bottleneck: Win B2B Sales More Often By Applying The The-ory   Of   Constraints.   https://www.forbes.com/councils/forbestechcoun-cil/2021/11/17/bust-the-bottleneck-win-b2b-sales-more-often-by-applying-thetheory-of-constraints/. Accessed 27 Aug 2024

8. Blocker CP, Cannon JP, Panagopoulos NG et al. (2012) The Role of Sales Force in Value Creation and Appropriation: New Directions for Research. Journal of Personal Selling & Sales Management 32:15–27. https://doi.org/10.2307/23483339

9. Storbacka K (2011) A solution business model: Capabilities and management practic-es for   integrated   solutions.   Industrial   Marketing   Management   40:699–711. https://doi.org/10.1016/j.indmarman.2011.05.003

10. Töytäri P, Rajala R (2015) Value- based selling: An organizational capability perspec-tive. Industrial Marketing Management 45:101–112

11. Huang K, Xie A (2023) Overview of ChatGPT, Web3, and New Business Landscape. In: Huang K, Wang Y, Zhu F et al. (eds) Beyond AI. Springer Nature Switzerland, Cham, pp 3–36

12. Wolf V, Maier C (2024) ChatGPT usage in everyday life: A motivation-theoretic mixed-methods   study.   International   Journal   of   Information   Management. https://doi.org/10.1016/j.ijinfomgt.2024.102821

13. Kulkarni A, Shivananda A, Kulkarni A et al. (2023) Applied Generative AI for Beginners. Apress, Berkeley, CA

14. Ertel W (2017) Introduction to Artificial Intelligence, 2nd edn. Springer International Publishing, Cham

15. Dwivedi YK, Kshetri N, Hughes L et al. (2023) Opinion Paper: "So what if ChatGPT wrote it " Multidisciplinary perspectives on opportunities, challenges and implica-tions of generative conversational AI for research, practice and policy. International Journal of Information Management

16. Fui-Hoon Nah F, Zheng R, Cai J et al. (2023) Generative AI and ChatGPT: Applica-tions, challenges, and AI-human collaboration. Journal of Information Technology Case and   Application   Research   25:277–304. https://doi.org/10.1080/15228053.2023.2233814

17. Dutt D, Amman B, Perricos C et al. (2024) Now decides next: Insights from the leading edge of generative AI adoption

18. Rigon G, Mullen A, Litan A et al. (2023) Best Practices for the Responsible Use of Natural Language Technologies

19. Engels R, Tolido R, Slatter M et al. (2023) Harnessing the potential of genAI: Top use cases   across   industries.   https://prod.ucwe.capgemini.com/wp-content/up-loads/2023/07/Final-Web-Version-Report-Harnessing-the-Value-of-GenAI.1.pdf. Ac-cessed 06 Jul 2024

20. Cooper HM (1988) Organizing Knowledge Syntheses: A Taxonomy of Literature Re-views. Knowledge in Society 1:104–126. https://doi.org/10.1007/BF03177550

21. Kitchenham B, Charters S (2007) Guidelines for Performing Systematic Literature Re-views in Software Engineering. Technical Report EBSE 2

22. Kitchenham B, Pearl Brereton O, Budgen D et al. (2009) Systematic literature re-views in software engineering – A systematic literature review. Information and Software Technology 51:7–15. https://doi.org/10.1016/j.infsof.2008.09.009
23. Fink A (2005) Conducting research literature reviews: From the Internet to paper, 2nd edn. SAGE Publications, Thousand Oaks, Calif.
24. Cooper H (1986) The Integrative Research Review: A Systematic Approach. Sage Publications: Beverly Hills, 1984, 143 pp. Educational Researcher 15:4–31
25. Mayring P (2014) Qualitative Content Analysis: Theoretical Foundation, Basic Procedures and Software Solution. SSOAR, Klagenfurt
26. Mayring P, Fenzl T (2014) Qualitative Inhaltsanalyse. In: Baur N, Blasius J, a.o. (eds) Handbuch Methoden der empirischen Sozialforschung. Springer VS, Wiesbaden, pp 543–556
27. Mayring P (2000) Qualitative Content Analysis. Forum Qualitative Sozialforschung / Forum: Qualitative Social Research, Vol 1, No 2 (2000): Qualitative Methods in Various Disciplines I: Psychology. https://doi.org/10.17169/fqs-1.2.1089
28. Helfferich C (2011) Die Qualität qualitativer Daten: Manual für die Durchführung qualitativer Interviews, 4. Auflage. SpringerLink Bücher. VS Verlag für Sozialwissenschaften, Wiesbaden
29. Züll C, Menold N (2014) Offene Fragen. In: Baur N, Blasius J, a.o. (eds) Handbuch Methoden der empirischen Sozialforschung. Springer VS, Wiesbaden, pp 713–719

Industry Track

A Future Impetus for the Automotive Industry

Alexander Rossmann[1]

[1] Reutlingen University, Herman Hollerith Zentrum, Reutlingen 72762, Germany
alexander.rossmann@reutlingen-university.de

Abstract. The first part of the Industry Track at HHC24 explored the future of the automotive industry, emphasizing the impact of artificial intelligence (AI) and software-defined vehicles. Presentations by Jan Wehinger (MHP - A Porsche Company) and Steffen Krause (Capgemini) highlighted key trends such as connected cars, advanced driver assistance systems (ADAS), and generative AI (GenAI) integration into embedded vehicle architectures. Krause's presentation, "Natural Language meets Embedded Code: Autosar and GenAI," examined the challenges of implementing GenAI in vehicle IT systems, which must balance real-time constraints, safety requirements, and cloud-based software agility. Wehinger's presentation, "Automotive Disruption: From Software-Defined Vehicle to Software-Defined Company," analyzed AI's transformative role across the automotive value chain. He emphasized AI as a disruptive force comparable to mobile internet and cloud computing.

Zusammenfassung. Der erste Teil des Industry Tracks auf der HHC24 untersuchte die Zukunft der Automobilindustrie und betonte die Auswirkungen von Künstlicher Intelligenz (KI) und softwaredefinierten Fahrzeugen. Die Präsentationen von Jan Wehinger (MHP - A Porsche Company) und Steffen Krause (Capgemini) beleuchteten zentrale Trends wie vernetzte Fahrzeuge, Advanced Driver Assistance Systems (ADAS) und die Integration von Generativer KI (GenAI) in eingebettete Fahrzeugarchitekturen. Krauses Vortrag „Natural Language meets Embedded Code: Autosar and GenAI" untersuchte die Herausforderungen der Implementierung von GenAI in Fahrzeug-IT-Systemen, die Echtzeitanforderungen, Sicherheitsvorgaben und agile Softwareentwicklung in Einklang bringen müssen. Wehingers Vortrag „Automotive Disruption: From Software-Defined Vehicle to Software-Defined Company" analysierte die transformative Rolle der KI entlang der automobilen Wertschöpfungskette.

Keywords: Automotive Industry, Software-defined Vehicle, Generative AI.

© Der/die Autor(en), exklusiv lizenziert an
Springer Fachmedien Wiesbaden GmbH, ein Teil von Springer Nature 2025
M. Möhring et al. (Hrsg.), *Herman Hollerith Conference 2024*, Informatik aktuell,
https://doi.org/10.1007/978-3-658-48215-2_11

1   Overview of Industry Track 1

The first part of the Industry Track at HHC24 deals with future impetus for the automotive industry. This part was supported by presentations from Jan Wehinger (MHP - A Porsche Company) and Steffen Krause (Capgemini). The following abstract contains a summary of the two presentations.

In general, the automotive industry is characterized by trends such as software-defined vehicles, connected cars, assistance systems and autonomous driving. Vehicles of the future must support an end-to-end IT architecture from electronic control units (ECUs) and embedded systems to a suitable middleware and the integration of services from the cloud. With this in mind, Steffen Krause's presentation on "Natural Language meets Embedded Code: Autosar and GenAI" deals with the integration of generative artificial intelligence into traditionally embedded systems as we know them from hardware-oriented vehicle architectures.

Generative artificial intelligence has grown to an omnipresent artifact in everyday lives via prominent solutions such as ChatGPT and Gemini [3,4,7]). However, the question is whether such solutions can be implemented in complex vehicle IT architectures [5]. The software systems of modern vehicles are characterized by several million lines of code [8]. Different programming languages and architecture models are used. This trend will be further intensified by Advanced Driving Assistance Systems (ADAS) in future. The integration of new services into this software stack is not trivial. In particular, the development of software in the context of cloud services differs significantly from hardware-centric software. Typical delivery models with continuous improvement via agile development, automated testing and frequent deployments are difficult in the vehicle sector. However, traditional development methods for vehicles look different. Feature requests often have to be planned for the long term and their impact on other functions needs tob e checked. In particular, safety-critical applications require long update cycles via safety tests and homologation.

Therefore, it is obvious that different development paradigms, methods and IT architectures collide when using Generative Artificial Intelligence (GenAI) in vehicles. De facto standards such as Autosar provide frameworks, specifications and interfaces for programming ECUs for many OEMs. For this purpose, software components are specified and flashed into ECUs as real-time-capable code. With more than 100 ECUs per vehicle and thousands of vehicles in the field, this quickly leads to considerable complexity. In future, the aim will be to synchronize embedded software in the field with cloud-based services. The challenge is to further develop such software in an agile manner while maintaining the requirements for safety and real-time capability.

The final result of model-based software development is flashed into ECUs in the form of a runtime environment in accordance with the Autosar framework. The question is how GenAI can be used to support model-based software development using AI. Such a development environment is based on different components: This includes (1) a traditional formulation of requirements, (2) a development environment for code generation, (3) prompt engineering for for addressing GenAI and (4) an agent system for analyzing the prompt and accessing a prepared database through Retrieval Augmented Generation (RAG) architectures. In this sense, a prepared database of Autosar artifacts is used as a knowledge base to significantly accelerate GenAI's model-driven software development for the Autosar framework.

The presentation of Jan Wehinger with the title „Automotive Disruption: From Software Defined Vehicle to Software Defined Company" also highlights the impact of Artificial Intelligence (AI) for the automotive industry (Slama, Nonnenmacher, and Irawan 2023). Thereby, Wehinger provides an in-depth analysis of the transformative potential of AI across the automotive value chain, from development and production to in-vehicle applications [6]. The presentation emphasizes that AI represents the next significant platform shift, comparable to the advent of mobile internet and cloud computing, and underscores the necessity for automotive companies to adopt a strategic approach to AI integration to maintain competitiveness [2].

Despite the recognized potential of AI, the automotive industry has been relatively cautious in its investments compared to other sectors. Only 30% of automotive companies have dedicated teams and budgets for AI initiatives, lagging behind industries such as retail and high-tech manufacturing. This hesitancy is attributed to uncertainties regarding implementation strategies and return on investment.

Wehinger cites insights from an international survey of 4,700 participants across China, the US, Germany, the UK, Italy, Sweden, and Poland, revealing significant regional differences in consumer attitudes toward AI in vehicles [1]. In Europe, 79% of respondents express interest in AI-supported vehicle functions, yet only 23% are willing to pay extra for these features. In contrast, 39% of Chinese consumers are open to additional charges for AI functionalities. Furthermore, while 80% of Chinese respondents understand AI systems in vehicles, only 54% of Europeans report similar comprehension, indicating a need for increased transparency and education in certain markets.

Moreover, traditional automotive manufacturers enjoy a higher level of trust regarding AI integration compared to technology firms. Approximately 64% of consumers trust established car manufacturers with AI development, whereas only 50% extend the same trust to tech companies like Apple, Google, and Microsoft. This trust advantage positions traditional manufacturers favorably for leading AI adoption in the automotive sector.

Wehinger offers seven key recommendations for automotive companies to effectively implement AI:

- Prioritize Digitalization: Ensure comprehensive digitalization and access to relevant data, as these are critical for successful AI solutions.
- Organizational Change: Establish clear responsibilities and competencies within the organization to assess and realize AI potential.
- Use Case Development: Focus on specific, evaluated use cases to guide AI application, avoiding implementation without clear objectives.
- Build Expertise: Develop teams with ongoing expertise in AI to evaluate market developments and adapt strategies accordingly.
- Ethical Considerations: Address ethical, legal, and security concerns pro-actively to build consumer trust and comply with regulations.
- Monetization Strategies: Explore both direct and indirect monetization avenues for AI offerings, such as data-based business models and enhanced services.
- Collaborative Partnerships: Engage in partnerships with technology providers and other stakeholders to leverage external expertise and accelerate AI integration.

By following these recommendations, automotive companies can harness AI's potential to drive innovation, improve efficiency, and enhance the overall customer experience, thereby securing a competitive edge in the evolving automotive landscape.

Both presentations show how AI supports the development of software in vehicles and what role AI can play in differentiating services in vehicles in the future. In this respect, the track offers relevant insights for companies and for further research into the integration of AI into key topics of vehicle development.

Acknowledgement: We thank all of the speakers and supporters of the industry track of the HHC. The chapter was based on the insights of the first track of the industry track based on the speaker's insights.

References

1. Friedel, Augustin, Marcus Willand, Matthias Borch, and Nils Schaupensteiner (2024), "Game-Changer KI: Die neue treibende Kraft der Automobilindustrie," https://www.mhp.com/de/insights/was-wir-denken/game-changer-ki-die-neue-treibende-kraft-der-automobilindustrie/, MHP, last accessed 2025/01/16
2. Garidis, Konstantin, Leon Ulbricht, Alexander Rossmann, and Marco Schmäh (2020), "Toward a user acceptance model of autonomous driving," in Proceedings of the 53rd Hawaii international conference on system sciences.
3. Hildebrand, Christian and Anouk Bergner (2019), "AI-Driven Sales Automation: Using Chatbots to Boost Sales.," NIM Marketing Intelligence Review, 11 (2), 36–41.
4. Jiang, Hua, Yang Cheng, Jeongwon Yang, and Shanbing Gao (2022), "AI-powered chatbot communication with customers: Dialogic interactions, satisfaction, engagement, and customer behavior," COMPUTERS IN HUMAN BEHAVIOR, 134.

5. Jovanovic, Marin, David Sjodin, and Vinit Parida (2022), "Co-evolution of platform architecture, platform services, and platform governance: Expanding the platform value of industrial digital platforms," TECHNOVATION, 118.

6. Langley, David J, Jenny van Doorn, Irene C L Ng, Stefan Stieglitz, Alexander Lazovik, and Albert Boonstra (2021), "The Internet of Everything: Smart things and their impact on business models," Journal of Business Research, 122, 853–63.

7. Rossmann, Alexander, Alfred Zimmermann, and Dieter Hertweck (2020), "The Impact of Chatbots on Customer Service Performance BT - Advances in the Human Side of Service Engineering," J. Spohrer and C. Leitner, eds., Cham: Springer International Publishing, 237–43.

8. Slama, Dirk, Achim Nonnenmacher, and Thomas Irawan (2023), "The Software-Defined Vehicle: A Digital-First Approach to Creating Next-Generation Experiences,", O'Reilly.

Practical support for regional SMEs from the AI Lab Stuttgart

Lukas Weiss[1,3] and Christine Schaller[2]

[1] AI-Lab Stuttgart for SMEs, HHZ, Reutlingen University, Reutlingen 72762, Germany
[2] AI-Lab Stuttgart for SMEs, ZD.BB GmbH, Böblingen 71034, Germany
[3] University of the West of Scotland, Paisley PA1 2BE, UK
Lukas.Weiss@Reutlingen-University.DE
christine.schaller@zd-bb.de

Abstract. The AI Lab Region of Stuttgart helps small and medium-sized enterprises (SMEs) and start-ups to get started with artificial intelligence (AI) quickly. Also, it helps improve the AI adoption process within these SMEs. This includes the availability of demonstrators, individual support from independent experts from the Faculty of Computer Science at Reutlingen University, various specialist seminars, practical workshops, and events on AI.

Keywords: AI adoption, support SMEs, AI demonstrator.

1 Summary of the activities of the AI Lab of Stuttgart

The KI-Lab Region Stuttgart supports SMEs and start-ups quickly, starting with AI. It offers practical AI use cases for your own company in production, logistics, marketing, market research, management, AI demonstrators for object recognition and energy consumption, and an AI knowledge store, including a technical development environment.

Various AI demonstrators are available on-site at the AI Lab Stuttgart. In addition, a knowledge repository for machine learning can be used online, which provides different data and AI models on a centralized platform. Over 20 use cases from various industries and business areas are available to get started with AI. A technical environment designated the "Machine Learning Sandbox," has been developed to experiment, develop, and test machine learning models and algorithms [1]. This environment is accessible via the website at www.ki-lab-region-stuttgart.de/praxisbeispiele and allows entrepreneurs and developers to comprehend and directly implement various AI applications.

These services were developed in the "Quick Start Artificial Intelligence at the AI Lab Stuttgart" project, funded by the Baden-Württemberg Ministry of Economic Affairs, Labor and Tourism. AI offers a wide range of potential, such as optimizing central value-adding processes or providing enhanced customer service. Machine learning enables computers to learn from data and constantly improve themselves without explicitly programming each instruction. Algorithms recognize specific patterns, make predictions, and automate decisions that become increasingly precise over time.

1.1   AI demonstrator: Energy consumption – HollerithEnergyML

The HollerithEnergyML[2] prototype was developed as a demonstrator for the Stuttgart AI Lab by the Herman Hollerith Center. The demonstrator is a machine learning system recommender that provides energy consumption when training various AI models. The web-based system helps to analyze and predict energy consumption for different AI models based on numerical and categorical features and data set size. The prototype supports SMEs in making energy-efficient decisions and saving energy in the long term. HollerithEnergyML is still in the development phase but already offers valuable predictions.

Fig. 1. AI Lab Stuttgart trade fair booth - HollerithEnergyML and AI object recognition demonstrators from the AI Lab Stuttgart.

1.2   AI demonstrator: object recognition is the simple route to take

Another innovative prototype for object recognition at the AI Lab Stuttgart shows how modern computer vision technologies can be used in everyday life [3]. With the help of a high-resolution webcam, the demonstrator recognizes various objects in real-time. The recognized objects are displayed on the screen and named by voice output. The system indicates the probability with which it has recognized the object. YOLOv8, a state-of-the-art computer vision model, is at the system's heart. This model can be used to identify objects quickly and precisely. The prototype is particularly suitable for the low-threshold visualization of computer vision and AI models. The combination of visual and acoustic feedback makes using these technologies intuitive and tangible.

1.3   About the KI-Lab Region Stuttgart and current facts and services

The AI Lab Stuttgart offers many support services to help companies start quickly with artificial intelligence. It is explicitly aimed at SMEs and start-ups from the region that want to utilize the potential of artificial intelligence. In addition, the AI Lab Stuttgart is constantly analyzing the problems of local SMEs concerning the application and introduction, and thus the adoption, of AI. In the process, an effort is made to adapt the services in and around the SME consultations to enable them to adopt AI technology in the best possible way. The AI Lab Stuttgart has already reached over 600 participants from companies and start-ups in the area. In addition to providing specialist knowledge in courses with over 120 participants or via demonstrators, the KI-Lab also actively supports implementing specific AI projects. The AI Lab Stuttgart has already offered support in over 55 individual consulting sessions, ranging from general AI application options to specific technical questions and projects. ZD.BB GmbH, Zentrum für Digitalisierung Landkreis Böblingen, coordinates the activities of the AI Lab Stuttgart. Support for AI and the technical content is provided in close cooperation with Reutlingen University at the Herman Hollerith Center in Böblingen. The AI Lab Stuttgart receives support from the Böblingen district and the Baden-Württemberg Ministry of Economic Affairs, Labor and Tourism.

References

1. KI-Lab Region Stuttgart: Praxisbeispiele, https://www.ki-lab-region-stuttgart.de/praxis-beispiele/, last accessed 2024/11/12.
2. Zanger, M., Schulz, A., Grodmeier, L., Agaj, D., Schindler, R., Weiss, L., Möhring, M.: HollerithEnergyML: a prototype of a machine learning energy consumption recommender system. In: Informatik 2024, pp. 1519–1523. Gesellschaft für Informatik eV (2024)
3. KI-Lab Region Stuttgart, https://www.ki-lab-region-stuttgart.de, last accessed 2024/11/12.

Author Index

Baharestani, Soufinaz 52
Breitenbücher, Uwe 1

Dahal, Keshav 18

Fink, Robin 42

Härer, Florian 28

Jungman, Dominic 74

Khan, Ali Umair 7
Koç, Hasan 52
Kudryavtsev, Dmitry 7

Laatikainen, Elisa 7

Moilanen, Teemu 7
Möhring, Michael 1, 18

Petrik, Dimitri 28, 63
Polat, Ebru 63

Roling, Bastian 63
Rossmann, Alexander 102

Sauter, Victoria 87
Schaller, Christine 107
Schlegel, Dennis 42
Schmidt, Rainer 4
Schöllkopf, Felix 28

Trieflinger, Stefan 63

Weiss, Lukas 18, 107

Zimmermann, Alfred 1

The manufacturer's authorised representative in the EU is Springer
Nature Customer Service Centre GmbH, Europaplatz 3, 69115 Heidelberg,
Germany. If you have any concerns regarding our products, please
contact ProductSafety@springernature.com

Printed and bound by CPI Group (UK) Ltd, Croydon, CR0 4YY

24/04/2026

02096366-0005